Arlo Bates

Talks on the Study of Literature

Arlo Bates

Talks on the Study of Literature

ISBN/EAN: 9783337205072

Printed in Europe, USA, Canada, Australia, Japan

Cover: Foto ©Thomas Meinert / pixelio.de

More available books at **www.hansebooks.com**

Books by Arlo Bates.

THE PHILISTINES. A Novel. 12mo, $1.50.
THE PAGANS. A Novel. 16mo, $1.00.
PATTY'S PERVERSITIES. A Novel. 16mo, $1.00; paper, 50 cents.
TALKS ON WRITING ENGLISH. Crown 8vo, $1.50.
TALKS ON THE STUDY OF LITERATURE. Crown 8vo, $1.50.

HOUGHTON, MIFFLIN & CO.
BOSTON AND NEW YORK.

TALKS

ON

THE STUDY OF LITERATURE

BY

ARLO BATES

BOSTON AND NEW YORK
HOUGHTON, MIFFLIN AND COMPANY
The Riverside Press, Cambridge
1897

1897
BY ARLO BATES
ALL RIGHTS RESERVED

THIS volume is made up from a course of lectures delivered under the auspices of the Lowell Institute in the autumn of 1895. These have been revised and to some extent rewritten, and the division into chapters made; but there has been no essential change.

CONTENTS

		PAGE
I.	What Literature Is	1
II.	Literary Expression	23
III.	The Study of Literature	33
IV.	Why we Study Literature	45
V.	False Methods	60
VI.	Methods of Study	69
VII.	The Language of Literature	88
VIII.	The Intangible Language	111
IX.	The Classics	123
X.	The Value of the Classics	135
XI.	The Greater Classics	142
XII.	Contemporary Literature	154
XIII.	New Books and Old	167
XIV.	Fiction	184
XV.	Fiction and Life	199
XVI.	Poetry	219
XVII.	The Texture of Poetry	227
XVIII.	Poetry and Life	241

TALKS ON THE STUDY OF LITERATURE

I

WHAT LITERATURE IS

As all life proceeds from the egg, so all discussion must proceed from a definition. Indeed, it is generally necessary to follow definition by definition, fixing the meaning of the terms used in the original explanation, and again explaining the words employed in this exposition.

I once heard a learned but somewhat pedantic man begin to answer the question of a child by saying that a lynx is a wild quadruped. He was allowed to get no further, but was at once asked what a quadruped is. He responded that it is a mammal with four feet. This of course provoked the inquiry what a mammal is; and so on from one question to another, until the original subject was entirely lost sight of, and the lynx disappeared in a maze of verbal distinctions as completely as it might have vanished in the tangles of the forest primeval. I feel that I am not wholly safe from danger of repeating the experience of this well-meaning pedant if I attempt to give a definition of literature. The temptation is strong to content myself with saying: "Of course we all know what literature is." The difficulty which I have had in the endeavor to frame a satisfactory explanation of the term has convinced me, however, that it is necessary to assume that few of us do know, and has impressed upon me the need of trying to make clear what the word means to me. If my statement seem insufficient for general application, it will at least show the sense which I shall give to "literature" in these talks.

In its most extended signification literature of course might be taken to include whatever is written or printed; but our concern is with that portion only which is indicated by the name "polite literature," or by the imported term "belles-lettres," — both antiquated though respectable phrases. In other words, I wish to confine my examination to those written works which can properly be brought within the scope of literature as one of the fine arts.

Undoubtedly we all have a general idea of the limitations which are implied by these various terms, and we are not without a more or less vague notion of what is indicated by the word literature in its most restricted and highest sense. The important point is whether our idea is clear and well realized. We have no difficulty in saying that one book belongs to art and that another does not; but we often find ourselves perplexed when it comes to telling why. We should all agree that "The Scarlet Letter" is literature and that the latest sensational novel is not, — but are we sure what makes the difference? We know that Shakespeare wrote poetry and Tupper doggerel, but it by no means follows that we can always distinguish doggerel from poetry; and while it is not perhaps of consequence whether we are able to inform others why we respect the work of one or another, it is of much importance that we be in a position to justify our tastes to ourselves. It is not hard to discover whether we enjoy a book, and it is generally possible to tell why we like it; but this is not the whole of the matter. It is necessary that we be able to estimate the justice of our preferences. We must remember that our liking or disliking is not only a test of the book, — but is a test of us as well. There is no more accurate gauge of the moral character of a man than the nature of the books which he really cares for. He who would progress by the aid of literature must have reliable standards by which to judge his literary feelings and opinions; he must be able to say: "My antipathy to such a work is justified by this or by that principle; my pleasure in that other is fine because for these reasons the book itself is noble."

It is hardly possible to arrive at any clear understanding of what is meant by literature as an art, without some conception of what constitutes art in general. Broadly speaking, art exists in consequence of the universal human desire for sympathy. Man is forever endeavoring to break down the wall which separates him from his fellows. Whether we call it egotism or simply humanity, we all know the wish to make others appreciate our feelings; to show them how we suffer, how we enjoy. We batter our fellow-men with our opinions sufficiently often, but this is as nothing to the insistence with which we pour out to them our feelings. A friend is the most valued of earthly possessions largely because he is willing to receive without appearance of impatience the unending story of our mental sensations. We are all of us more or less conscious of the constant impulse which urges us on to expression; of the inner necessity which moves us to continual endeavors to make others share our thoughts, our experiences, but most of all our emotions. It seems to me that if we trace this instinctive desire back far enough, we reach the beginnings of art.

It may seem that the splendidly immeasurable achievements of poetry and painting, of architecture, of music and sculpture, are far enough from this primal impulse; but I believe that in it is to be found their germ. Art began with the first embodiment of human feelings by permanent means. Let us suppose, by way of illustration, some prehistoric man, thrilled with awe and terror at sight of a mastodon, and scratching upon a bone rude lines in the shape of the animal, — not only to give information, not only to show what the beast was like, but also to convey to his fellows his feelings when confronted with the monster. It is as if he said: "See! I cannot put into words what I felt; but look! the creature was like this. Think how you would feel if you came face to face with it. Then you will know how I felt." Something of this sort may the beginnings of art be conceived to have been.

I do not mean, of course, that the prehistoric man who made such a picture — and such a picture exists — analyzed his motives. He felt a thing which he could not say in words; he instinctively turned to pictorial representation, — and graphic art was born.

The birth of poetry was probably not entirely dissimilar. Barbaric men, exulting in the wild delight of victory, may seem unlikely sponsors for the infant muse, and yet it is with them that song began. The savage joy of the conquerors, too great for word, found vent at first in excited, bounding leaps and uncouthly ferocious gestures, by repetition growing into rhythm; then broke into inarticulate sounds which timed the movements, until these in turn gave place to words, gradually moulded into rude verse by the measures of the dance. The need of expressing the feelings which swell inwardly, the desire of sharing with others, of putting into tangible form, the emotions that thrill the soul is common to all human beings; and it is from this that arises the thing which we call art.

The essence of art, then, is the expression of emotion; and it follows that any book to be a work of art must embody sincere emotion. Not all works which spring from genuine feeling succeed in embodying or conveying it. The writer must be sufficiently master of technique to be able to make words impart what he would express. The emotion phrased must moreover be general and in some degree typical. Man is interested and concerned in the emotions of men only in so far as these throw light on the nature and possibilities of life. Art must therefore deal with what is typical in the sense that it touches the possibilities of all human nature. If it concerns itself with much that only the few can or may experience objectively, it has to do with that only which all human beings may be conceived of as sharing subjectively. Literature may be broadly defined as the adequate expression of genuine and typical emotion. The definition may seem clumsy, and hardly exact enough to be allowed in theoretical æsthetics; but it seems to me sufficiently accurate to serve our present purpose. Certainly the essentials of literature are the adequate embodiment of sincere and general feeling.

By sincerity here we mean that which is not conventional, which is not theoretical, not artificial; that which springs from a desire honestly to impart to others exactly the emotion that has been actually felt. By the term "emotion" or "feeling" we mean those inner sensations of pleasure, excitement, pain, or passion, which are distinguished from the merely intellectual processes of the mind, — from thought, perception, and reason. It is not necessary to trespass just now on the domain of the psychologist by an endeavor to establish scientific distinctions. We are all able to appreciate the difference between what we think and what we feel, between those things which touch the intellect and those which affect the emotional nature. We see a sentence written on paper, and are intellectually aware of it; but unless it has for us some especial message, unless it concerns us personally, we are not moved by it. Most impressions which we receive touch our understanding without arousing our feelings. This is all so evident that there is not likely to arise in your minds any confusion in regard to the meaning of the phrase "genuine emotion."

Whatever be the origin of this emotion it must be essentially impersonal, and it is generally so in form. There are comparatively few works of art which are confessedly the record of simple, direct, personal experience; and perhaps none of these stand in the front rank of literature. Of course I am not speaking of literature which takes a personal form, like any book written in the first person; but of those that are avowedly a record of actual life. We must certainly include in literature works like the "Reflections" of Marcus Aurelius, the "Confessions" of Augustine, and — though the cry is far — Rousseau, and the "Journal Intime" of Amiel, but there is no one of these which is to be ranked high in the scale of the world's greatest books. Even in poetry the same thing is true. However we may admire "In Memoriam" and that much greater poem, Mrs. Browning's "Sonnets from the Portuguese," we are little likely to regard them as standing supremely high among the masterpieces. The "Sonnets" of Shakespeare which we suppose to be personal are yet with supreme art made so impersonal that as far as the reader is concerned the experiences which they record might be entirely imaginary. It is in proportion as a poet is able to give this quality which might be called generalization to his work that it becomes art.

The reason of this is not far to seek. If the emotion is professedly personal it appeals less strongly to mankind, and it is moreover likely to interfere with its own effective embodiment. All emotion in literature must be purely imaginative as far as its expression in words is concerned. Of course poetical form may be so thoroughly mastered as to become almost instinctive, but nevertheless acute personal feeling must trammel utterance. It is not that the author does not live through what he sets forth. It is that the artistic moment is not the moment of experience, but that of imaginative remembrance. The "Sonnets from the Portuguese" afford admirable examples of what I mean. It is well known that these relate a most completely personal and individual story. Not only the sentiments but the circumstances set forth were those of the poet's intimate actual life. It was the passion of love and of self-renunciation in her own heart which broke forth in the fine sonnet: —

> Go from me, yet I feel that I shall stand
> Henceforward in thy shadow. Nevermore
> Alone upon the threshold of the door

> Of individual life shall I command
> The uses of my soul; or lift my hand
>   Serenely in the sunshine as before
>   Without the sense of that which I forebore, —
> Thy touch upon the palm. The widest land
> Doom takes to part us, leaves thy heart in mine
>   With pulses that beat double. What I do
> And what I dream include thee, as the wine
>   Must taste of its own grapes: and when I sue
> God for myself, He hears that name of thine,
>   And sees within my eyes the tears of two.

There came to Mrs. Browning a poignant moment when she realized with a thrill of anguish what it would mean to her to live out her life alone, separated forever from the lover who had won her back from the very grasp of death. It was not in the pang of that throe that she made of it a sonnet; but afterward, while it was still felt, it is true, but felt rather as a memory vividly reproduced by the imagination. In so far both he who writes impersonally and he who writes personally are dealing with that which at the instant exists in the imagination. In the latter, however, there is still the remembrance of the actuality, the vibration of the joy or sorrow of which that imagining is born. Human self-consciousness intrudes itself whenever one is avowedly writing of self; sometimes even vanity plays an important part. From these and other causes it results that, whatever may be the exceptions, the highest work is that which phrases the general and the impersonal with no direct reference to self. Personal feeling lies behind all art, and no work can be great which does not rest on a basis of experience, more or less remotely; yet the greatest artist is he who embodies emotion, not in terms of his own life, but in those which make it equally the property of all mankind. It is feeling no longer egotistic, but broadly human. If the simile do not seem too homely, we might say that the difference is that between arithmetic and algebra. In the one case it is the working out of a particular problem; in the other of an equation which is universal.

Mankind tests art by universal experience. If an author has really felt what he has written, if what he sets down has been actual to him in imagination, whether actual in experience or not, readers recognize this, and receive his work, so that it lives. If he has affected a feeling, if he has shammed emotion, the whole is sure to ring false, and the world soon tires of his writings. Immediate popular judgment of a book is pretty generally wrong; ultimate general estimate is invariably correct. Humanity knows the truth of human feeling; and while it may be fooled for a time, it comes to the truth at last, in act if not in theory. The general public is guided by the wise few, and it does not reason out the difference between the genuine and the imitation; but it will in the end save the real, while the sham is forgotten through utter neglect.

Even where an author has seemingly persuaded himself that his pretended emotions are real, he cannot permanently deceive the world. You may remember the chapter in Aldrich's delightful

"Story of a Bad Boy" which relates how Tom Bailey, being crossed in love at the mature age of fourteen, deliberately became a "blighted being;" how he neglected his hair, avoided his playmates, made a point of having a poor appetite, and went mooning about forsaken graveyards, endeavoring to fix his thoughts upon death and self-destruction; how entirely the whole matter was a humbug, and yet how sincere the boy was in supposing himself to be unutterably melancholy. "It was a great comfort," he says, "to be so perfectly miserable and yet not to suffer any. I used to look in the glass and gloat over the amount and variety of mournful expression I could throw into my features. If I caught myself smiling at anything, I cut the smile short with a sigh. The oddest thing about all this is, I never once suspected that I was not unhappy. No one . . . was more deceived than I." We have all of us had experiences of this kind, and I fancy that there are few writers who cannot look back to a stage in their career when they thought that it was a prime essential of authorship to believe themselves to feel things which they did not feel in the least. This sort of self-deception is characteristic of a whole school of writers, of whom Byron was in his day a typical example. There is no doubt that Byron, greatly gifted as he was, took his mooning melancholy with monstrous seriousness when he began to write it, and the public received it with equal gravity. Yet Byron's mysterious misery, his immeasurable wickedness, his misanthropy too great for words, were mere affectations, — stage tricks which appealed to the gallery. Nobody is moved by them now. The fact that the poet himself thought that he believed in them could not save them. Byron had other and nobler qualities which make his best work endure, but it is in spite of his Bad-Boy-ish pose as a "blighted being." The fact is that sooner or later time tries all art by the tests of truth and common sense, and nothing which is not genuine is able to endure this proving.

To be literature a work must express sincere emotion; but how is feeling which is genuine to be distinguished from that which is affected? All that has been said must be regarded as simply theoretical and of very little practical interest unless there be some criterion by which this question may be settled. Manifestly we cannot so far enter into the consciousness of the writer as to tell whether he does or does not feel what he expresses; it can be only from outward signs that we judge whether his imagination has first made real to him what he undertakes to make real for others.

Something may be judged by the amount of seriousness with which a thing is written. The air of sincerity which is inevitable in the genuine is most difficult to counterfeit. What a man really feels he writes with a certain earnestness which may seem indefinite, but which is sufficiently tangible in its effects upon the reader. More than by any other single influence mankind has in all its history been more affected by the contagion of belief; and it is not easy to exaggerate the susceptibility of humanity to this force. Vague and elusive as this test of the genuineness of emotion might seem, it is in reality capable of much practical application. We have no trouble in deciding that the conventional rhymes which fill the corners of the newspapers are not the product of genuine inner stress. We are too well acquainted with these time-draggled rhymes of "love" and "dove," of "darts" and "hearts," of "woe" and "throe;" we have encountered too often these pretty, petty fancies, these twilight musings and midnight moans, this mild melancholy and maudlin sentimentality. We have only to read these trig little bunches of verse, tied up, as it were, with sad-colored ribbons, to feel their artificiality. On the other hand, it is impossible to read "Helen of Kirconnel," or Browning's "Prospice," or Wordsworth's poems to Lucy, without being sure that the poet meant that which he said in his song with all the fervor of heart and imagination. A reader need not be very critical to feel that the novels of the "Duchess" and her tribe are made by a process as mechanical as that of making paper flowers; he will not be able to advance far in literary judgment without coming to suspect that fiction like the pleasant pot-boilers of William Black and W. Clark Russell, if hand-made, is yet manufactured according to an arbitrary pattern; but what reader can fail to feel that to Hawthorne "The Scarlet Letter" was utterly true, that to Thackeray Colonel Newcome was a creature warm with human blood and alive with a vigorous humanity? Theoretically we may doubt our power to judge of the sincerity of an author, but we do not find this so impossible practically.

Critics sometimes say of a book that it is or is not "convincing." What they mean is that the author has or has not been able to make what he has written seem true to the imagination of the reader. The man who in daily life attempts to act a part is pretty sure sooner or later to betray himself to the observant eye. His real self will shape the disguise under which he has hidden it; he may hold out the hands and say the words of Esau, but the voice with which he speaks will perforce be the voice of Jacob. It is so in literature, and especially in literature which arouses the perceptions by an appeal to the imagination. The writer must be in earnest himself or he cannot convince the reader. To the man who invents a fiction, for instance, the story which he has devised must in his imagination be profoundly true or it will not be true to the audience which he addresses. To the novelist who is "convincing," his characters are as real as the men he meets in his walks or sits beside at table. It is for this reason that every novelist with imagination is likely to find that the fictitious personages of his story seem to act independently of the will of the author. They are so real that they must follow out the laws of their character, although that character exists only in imagination. For the author to feel this verity in what he writes is of course not all that is needed to enable him to convince his public; but it is certain that he is helpless without it, and that he cannot make real to others what is not real to himself.

In emotion we express the difference between the genuine and the counterfeit by the words "sentiment" and "sentimentality." Sentiment is what a man really feels; sentimentality is what he persuades himself that he feels. The Bad Boy as a "blighted being" is the type of sentimentalists for all time. There is about the same relation between sentimentality and sentiment that there is between a paper doll and the lovely girl that it represents. There are fashions in emotions as there are fashions in bonnets; and foolish mortals are as prone to follow one as another. It is no more difficult for persons of a certain quality of mind to persuade themselves that they thrill with what they conceive to be the proper emotion than it is for a woman to convince herself of the especial fitness to her face of the latest device in utterly unbecoming headgear. Our grandmothers felt that proper maidenly sensibility required them to be so deeply moved by tales of broken hearts and unrequited affection that they must escape from the too poignant anguish by fainting into the arms of the nearest man. Their grandchildren to-day are neither more nor less sincere, neither less nor more sensible in following to extremes other emotional modes which it might be invidious to specify. Sentimentality will not cease while the power of self-deception remains to human beings.

With sentimentality genuine literature has no

more to do than it has with other human weaknesses and vices, which it may picture but must not share. With sentiment it is concerned in every line. Of sentiment no composition can have too much; of sentimentality it has more than enough if there be but the trace shown in a single affectation of phrase, in one unmeaning syllable or unnecessary accent.

There are other tests of the genuineness of the emotion expressed in literature which are more tangible than those just given; and being more tangible they are more easily applied. I have said that sham sentiment is sure to ring false. This is largely due to the fact that it is inevitably inconsistent. Just as a man has no difficulty in acting out his own character, whereas in any part that is assumed there are sure sooner or later to be lapses and incongruities, so genuine emotion will be consistent because it is real, while that which is feigned will almost surely jar upon itself. The fictitious personage that the novelist actually shapes in his imagination, that is more real to him than if it stood by his side in solid flesh, must be consistent with itself because it is in the mind of its creator a living entity. It may not to the reader seem winning or even human, but it will be a unit in its conception and its expression, a complete and consistent whole. The poem which comes molten from the furnace of the imagination will be a single thing, not a collection of verses more or less ingeniously dovetailed together. The work which has been felt as a whole, which has been grasped as a whole, which has as a whole been lived by that inner self which is the only true producer of art, will be so consistent, so unified, so closely knit, that the reader cannot conceive of it as being built up of fortuitous parts, or as existing at all except in the beautiful completeness which genius has given it.

What I mean may perhaps be more clear to you if you take any of the little tinkling rhymes which abound, and examine them critically. Even some of more merit easily afford example. Take that pleasant rhyme so popular in the youth of our fathers, "The Old Oaken Bucket," and see how one stanza or another might be lost without being missed, how one thought or another has obviously been put in for the rhyme or to fill out the verse, and how the author seems throughout always to have been obliged to consider what he might say next, putting his work together as a joiner matches boards for a table-top. Contrast this with the absolute unity of Wordsworth's "Daffodils," Keats' "Ode to a Grecian Urn," Shelley's "Stanzas Written in Dejection," or any really great lyric. You will perceive the difference better than any one can say it. It is true that the quality of which we are speaking is sufficiently subtile to make examples unsatisfactory and perhaps even dangerous; but it seems to me that it is not too much to say that any careful and intelligent reader will find little difficulty in feeling the unity of the masterpieces of literature.

This lack of consistency is most easily appreciated, perhaps, in the drawing of character. Those modern writers who look upon literature as having two functions, first, to advance extravagant theories, and second, — and more important, — to advertise the author, are constantly putting forward personages that are so inconsistent that it is impossible not to see that they are mere embodied arguments or sensationalism incarnate, and not in the least creatures of a strong and wholesome imagination. When in "The Doll's House" Ibsen makes Nora Helma an inconsequent, frivolous, childish puppet, destitute alike of moral and of common sense, and then in the twinkling of an eye transforms her into an indignant woman, full of moral purpose, furnished not only with a complete set of advanced views but with an entire battery of modern arguments with which to support them, — when, in a word, the author, for the sake of his theory, works a visible miracle, we cease to believe in his imaginative sincerity. We know that he is dogmatizing, not creating; that this is artifice, not art.

Another test of the genuineness of what is expressed in literature is its truth to life. Here again we tread upon ground somewhat uncertain, since truth is as elusive as a sunbeam, and to no two human beings the same. Yet while the meaning of life is not the same to any two who walk under the heavens, there are certain broad principles which all men recognize. The eternal facts of life and of death, of love and of hate, the instinct of self-preservation, the fear of pain, the respect for courage, and the enthrallment of passion, —

these are laws of humanity so universal that we assume them to be known to all mankind. We cannot believe that any mortal can find that true to his imagination which ignores these unvarying conditions of human existence. He who writes what is untrue to humanity cannot persuade us that he writes what is true to himself. We are sure that those impossible heroes of Ouida, with their superhuman accomplishments, those heroines of beauty transcendently incompatible with their corrupt hearts, base lives, and entire defiance of all sanitary laws, were no more real to their author than they are to us. Conviction springs from the imagination, and imagination is above all else the realizing faculty. It is idle to say that a writer imagines every extravagant and impossible whimsy which comes into his head. He imagines those things, and those things only, which are real to his inner being; so that in judging literature the question to be settled is: Does this thing which the author tells, this emotion which he expresses, impress us as having been to him when he wrote actual, true, and absolutely real? To unimaginative persons it might seem that I am uttering nonsense. It is not possible for a man without imagination to see how things which are invented by the mind should by that same mind, in all sanity, be received as real. Yet that is precisely what happens. No one, I believe, produces real or permanent literature who is not capable of performing this miracle; who does not feel to be true that which has no other being, no other place, no other significance save that which it derives from the creative power of his own inner sense, working upon the material furnished by his perception of the world around him. This is the daily miracle of genius; but it is a miracle shared to some extent by every mortal who has the faintest glimmer of genuine imagination.

To be convincing literature must express emotion which is genuine; to commend itself to the best sense of mankind, and thus to take its place in the front rank, it must deal with emotion which is wholesome and normal. A work phrasing morbid emotion may be art, and it may be lasting; but it is not the highest art, and it does not approve itself to the best and sanest taste. Mankind looks to literature for the expression of genuine, strong, healthy human emotion; emotion passionate, tragic, painful, the exhilaration of joy or the frenzy of grief, as it may be; but always the emotion which under the given conditions would be felt by the healthy heart and soul, by the virile man and the womanly woman.)No amount of insane power flashing here and there amid the foulness of Tolstoi's "Kreutzer Sonata," can reconcile the world to the fact that the book embodies the broodings of a mind morbid and diseased. Even to concede that the author of such a work had genius could not avail to conceal the fact that his muse was smitten from head to feet with the unspeakable corruption of leprosy. Morbid literature may produce a profound sensation, but it is incapable of creating a permanent impression.

The principles of which we are speaking are strikingly illustrated in the tales of Edgar Allan Poe. He was possessed of an imagination narrow, but keen; uncertain and wayward, but alert and swift; individual and original, though unhappily lacking any ethical stability. In his best work he is sincere and convincing, so that stories like "The Cask of Amontillado," "The Gold Bug," or "The Purloined Letter," are permanently effective, each in its way and degree. Poe's masterpiece, "The Fall of the House of Usher," is a study of morbid character, but it is saved by the fact that this is viewed in its effect upon a healthy nature. The reader looks at everything through the mind of the imaginary narrator, so that the ultimate effect is that of an exhibition of the feelings of a wholesome nature brought into contact with madness; although even so the ordinary reader is still repelled by the abnormal elements of the theme. There is in all the work of Poe a good deal that is fantastic and not a little that is affected. He is rarely entirely sincere and sane. He shared with Byron an instinctive fondness for the rôle of a "blighted being," and a halo of inebriety too often encircles his head; yet at his best he moves us by the mysterious and incommunicable power of genius. Many of his tales, on the other hand, are mere mechanical tasks, and as such neither convincing nor permanent. There is a great deal of Poe which is not worth anybody's reading because he did not believe it, did not imagine it as real, when he wrote it. Other stories of his illustrate the futility of self-deception on the part of the author. "Lygeia" Poe always announced as his masterpiece. He apparently persuaded himself that he felt its turgid sentimentality, that he thrilled at its elaborately theatrical setting, and he flattered himself that he could cheat the world as he had cheated himself. Yet the reader is not fooled. Every man of judgment realizes that, however the author was able to deceive himself, "Lygeia" is rubbish, and sophomoric rubbish at that.

There has probably never before been a time which afforded so abundant illustrations of morbid work as to-day. We shall have occasion later to speak of Verlaine, Zola, Ibsen, and the rest, with their prurient prose and putrescent poetry; and here it is enough to note that the diseased and the morbid are by definition excluded from literature in the best sense of the word. Good art is not only sincere; it is human, and wholesome, and sound.

II

LITERARY EXPRESSION

So much, then, for what literature must express; it is well now to examine for a little the manner of expression. To feel genuine emotion is not all that is required of a writer. Among artists cannot be reckoned

> One born with poet's heart in sad eclipse
> Because unmatched with poet's tongue;
> Whose song impassioned struggles to his lips,
> Yet dies, alas! unsung.

He must be able to sing the song; to make the reader share the throbbing of his heart. All men feel; the artist is he who can by the use of conventions impart his feelings to the world. The musician uses conventions of sound, the painter conventions of color, the sculptor conventions of form, and the writer must employ the means most artificial of all, the conventions of language.

Here might be considered, if there were space, the whole subject of artistic technique; but it is sufficient for our purposes to notice that the test of technical excellence is the completeness with which the means are adapted to the end sought. The crucial question in regard to artistic workmanship is: "Does it faithfully and fully convey the emotion which is the essence of the work?" A work of art must make itself felt as well as intellectually understood; it must reach the heart as well as the brain. If a picture, a statue, a piece of music, or a poem provokes your admiration without touching your sensibilities, there is something radically wrong with the work — or with you.

First of all, then, expression must be adequate. If it is slovenly, incomplete, unskillful, it fails to impart the emotion which is its purpose. We have all sat down seething with excitement and endeavored to get our feelings upon paper, only to discover that our command of ourselves and of technical means was not sufficient to allow us to phrase adequately that which yet we felt most sincerely. It is true that style is in a sense a subordinate matter, but it is none the less an essential one. It is manifestly of little consequence to the world what one has to say if one cannot say it. We cannot be thrilled by the song which the dumb would sing had he but voice.

Yet it is necessary to remember that although expression must be adequate, it must also be subordinate. It is a means and not an end, and the least suspicion of its having been put first destroys our sense of the reality of the feeling it embodies. If an actress in moments of impassioned declamation is detected arranging her draperies, her art no longer carries conviction. Nobody feeling the heart-swelling words of Queen Katharine, for instance, could while speaking them be openly concerned about the effective disposition of her petticoats. The reader of too intricate and elaborate verse, such as the French forms of triolet, rondeau, rondel, and so on, has an instinctive perception that a poet whose attention was taken up with the involved and artfully difficult versification could not have been experiencing any deep passion, no matter how strongly the verse protests that he has. Expression obviously artful instantly arouses suspicion that it has been wrought for its own sake only.

Technical excellence which displays the cleverness of the artist rather than imparts the emotion which is its object, defeats its own end. A book so elaborated that we feel that the author was absorbed in perfection of expression rather than in what he had to express leaves us cold and unmoved, if it does not tire us. The messenger has usurped the attention which belonged to the message. It is not impossible that I shall offend some of you when I say that Walter Pater's "Marius the Epicurean" seems to me a typical example of this sort of book. The author has expended his energies in exquisite excesses of language; he has refined his style until it has become artfully inanimate. It is like one of the beautiful glass flowers in the Harvard Museum. It is not a living rose. It is no longer a message spoken to the heart of mankind; it is a brilliant exercise in technique.

Literature, then, is genuine emotion, adequately expressed. To be genuine it must come from the imagination; and adequate expression is that which in turn reaches the imagination. If it were not that the phrase seems forbiddingly cumbersome, we might, indeed, define literature as being such writings as are able to arouse emotion by an appeal to the imagination.

A sensational story, what the English call a "penny dreadful" or a "shilling shocker" according to the cost of the bundle of cheap excitement, may be an appeal to the emotions, but it aims to act upon the senses or the nerves. Its endeavor is to work by the grossest and most palpable means. It is an assault, so to say, upon the perceptions. Books of this sort have nothing to do with imagination, either in reader or writer. They would be ruled out by all the tests which we have given, since they are not sincere, not convincing, not consistent, not true to life.

One step higher in the scale come romances of abounding fancy, of which "She" may serve as an example. They are clever feats of intellectual jugglery, and it is to the intellectual perceptions that they appeal. Not, it is true, to the intellect in its loftiest moods, but the understanding as distinguished from the feeling. No reader is really moved by them. The ingenuity of the author amuses and absorbs the attention. The dexterity and unexpectedness of the tale excite and entertain. The pleasure experienced in reading these books is not far removed from that experienced in seeing a clever contortionist. To read them is like going to the circus, — a pleasant diversion, and one not without a certain importance to this overwrought generation. It is amusement, although not of a high grade.

Do not suppose, however, that I am saying that a story cannot have an exciting plot and yet be literature. In the restricted sense in which these lectures take the term, I should say that "The Adventures of Captain Horn," an agreeable book which has been widely read of late, is not literature; and yet "Treasure Island," upon which perhaps to some extent the former was modeled, most certainly is literature. The difference is that while Stockton in "Captain Horn" has worked with clever ingenuity to entertain, Stevenson in "Treasure Island" so vividly imagined what he wrote that he has made his characters human, informed every page with genuine feeling, and produced a romance permanently vital. The plot of those superb masterpieces of adventure, the "D'Artagnan Romances," is as wild, perhaps as extravagant, as that of the marrow-curdling tales which make the fortunes of sensational papers; but to the excitement of adventure is added that unification, that humanization, that perfection of imaginative realism which mark Dumas as a genius.

The difference of effect between books which are not literature and those which are is that while these amuse, entertain, glance over the surface of the mind, those touch the deepest springs of being. They touch us æsthetically, it is true. The emotion aroused is impersonal, and thus removed from the keen thrill which is born of actual experiences; but it depends upon the same passions, the same characteristics, the same humanity, that underlie the joys and sorrows of real life. It is because we are capable of passion and of disappointment that we are moved by the love and anguish of Romeo and Juliet, of Francesca and Paolo. Our emotion is not identical with that with which the heart throbs in personal love and grief; yet art which is genuine awakes emotion thoroughly genuine. Books of sensationalism and sentimentality may excite curiosity, or wonder, or amusement, or sham feeling; but they must have at least some spark of sacred fire before they can arouse in the intelligent reader this inner throb of real feeling.

The personal equation must be considered here. The same book must affect different readers differently. From the sentimental maid who weeps in the kitchen over "The Seventy Sorrows of Madelaine the Broken-hearted," to her master in his library, touched by the grief of King Lear, is indeed a far cry; and yet both may be deeply moved. It may be asked whether we have arrived at a standard which will enable us to judge between them.

The matter is perhaps to be cleared up somewhat by a little common sense. It is not hard to decide whether the kitchen-maid in question has an imagination sufficiently well developed to bring her within the legitimate grounds of inquiry; and the fiction which delights her rudimentary understanding is easily ruled out. It is not so easy, however, to dispose of this point entirely. There is always a border-land concerning which doubts and disagreements must continue to exist. In all matters connected with the feelings it is necessary to recognize the fact that the practical is not likely to accord fully with the theoretical. We define literature only to be brought face to face with the difficulty which is universal in art, the difficulty of degree. No book will answer, it may be, to a theoretical definition, no work conform completely to required conditions. The composition which is a masterpiece stands at one end of the list, and comes so near to the ideal that there is no doubt of its place. At the other end there is the rubbish, equally unquestioned in its worthlessness. The troublesome thing is to decide where between comes the dividing line above which is literature. We call a ring or a coin gold, knowing that it contains a mixture of alloy. The goldsmith may have a standard, and refuse the name gold to any mixture into which enters a given per cent of baser metal; but in art this is impossible. Here each reader must decide for himself. Whether works which lie near the line are to be considered literature is a question to be decided individually. Each reader is justified in making his own decision, provided only that he found it upon definite principles. It is largely a question what is one's own responsiveness to literature. There are those to whom Tolstoi's "War and Peace" is a work of greatness, while others fail to find it anything but a chaotic and unorganized note-book of a genius not self-responsible. "John Inglesant" appeals to many persons of excellent taste as a novel of permanent beauty, while to some it seems sentimental and artificial. Mr. Lowell and others have regarded Sylvester Judd's "Margaret" as one of the classics of American fiction; yet it has never appealed to the general public, and an eminent literary man told me not long ago that he finds it dull. To these and to all other varying opinions there is but one thing to be said: Any man has a right to his judgment if it is founded upon the logical application of definite principles. Any opinion which is sincere and based upon standards must be treated with respect, whether it is agreed with or not.

It is difficult, on the other hand, to feel that there is any moral excuse for prejudices which are the result of individual whims rather than of deliberate judgment. An opinion should not be some burr caught up by the garments unawares; but a fruit carefully selected as the best on the tree. The fact is that the effort of forming an intelligent judgment is more severe than most persons care to undertake unless absolutely forced to it. It sometimes seems as if the whole tendency of modern life were in the direction of cultivating mental dexterity until the need of also learning mental concentration is in danger of being overlooked. Men are trained to meet intellectual emergencies, but not to endure continued intellectual strain. The difficulty which is to be conquered by a sudden effort they are able to overcome, but when deliberation and continuous mental achievement are required, the weakness of their training is manifest. The men, and perhaps still more the women, of to-day are ready to decide upon the merits of a book in the twinkling of an eye; and it is to be acknowledged that these snap judgments are reasonable far more often than could have been expected. When it comes, however, to having a reason for the faith that is in them, it is lamentable how many intelligent persons prove utterly incapable of fairly and logically examining literature; and it must be conceded that there should be some other test by which to decide whether a book is to be included under the gracious name of literature than the dogmatic assertion: "Well, I don't care what anybody says against it; I like it!"

We have discussed the distinctions by which it may be decided what is to be considered literature; and, did space warrant, we might go on to examine the principles which determine the rank of work. They are of course largely to be inferred from what has been said already. The merit of literature will be chiefly dependent upon the closeness with which it conforms to the rules which mark the nature of literature. The more fully genuine its emotion, the more adequate its expression, the higher the scale in which a book is to be placed. The more sane and healthful, the more entirely in accord with the needs and springs of general human life, the greater the work. Indeed, beyond this there is little to say save that the nobility of intention, the ethical significance of the emotion embodied, mark the worth and the rank of a composition.

I have tried to define literature, and yet in the end my strongest feeling is that of the inadequacy of my definition. He would be but a lukewarm lover who was capable of framing a description which would appear to him to embody fully the perfections of his mistress; and art is a mistress so beautiful, so high, so noble, that no phrases can fitly characterize her, no service can be wholly worthy of her. Life is full of disappointment, and pain, and bitterness, and that sense of futility in which all these evils are summed up; and yet even were there no other alleviation, he who knows and truly loves literature finds here a sufficient reason to be glad that he lives. Science may show man how to live; art makes living worth his while. Existence to-day without literature would be a failure and a despair; and if we cannot satisfactorily define our art, we at least are aware how it enriches and ennobles the life of every human being who comes within the sphere of its wide and gracious influence.

III

THE STUDY OF LITERATURE

WHEN it is clearly understood what literature is, there may still remain a good deal of vagueness in regard to the study of it. It is by no means sufficient for intellectual development that one have a misty general share in the conventional respect traditionally felt for such study. There should be a clear and accurate comprehension why the study of literature is worth the serious attention of earnest men and women.

It might at first thought seem that of this question no discussion is needed. It is generally assumed that the entire matter is sufficiently obvious, and that this is all that there is to it. The obvious, however, is often the last to be perceived; and such is the delusiveness of human nature that to call a thing too plain to need demonstration is often but a method of concealing inability to prove. Men are apt to fail to perceive what lies nearest to them, while to cover their blindness and ignorance they are ready to accept without reasoning almost any assumption which comes well recommended. The demand for patent medicines, wide-spread as it is, is insignificant in comparison to the demand for ready-made opinions. Most men accept the general belief, and do not trouble themselves to make it really theirs by examining the grounds upon which it is based. We all agree that it is well to study literature, it is probable; but it is to be feared that those of us who can say exactly why it is well do not form a majority.

The word "study," it may be remarked in passing, is not an entirely happy one in this connection. It has, it is true, many delightful associations, especially for those who have really learned how to study; but it has, too, a certain doleful suggestiveness which calls up painful memories of childhood. It is apt to bring to mind bitter hours when some example in long division stood like an impassable wall between us and all happiness; when complex fractions deprived life of all joy, or the future was hopelessly blurred by being seen through a mist of tears and irregular French verbs. The word "study" is therefore likely to seem to indicate a mechanical process, full of weariness and vexation of spirit. This is actually true of no study which is worthy of the name; and least of all is it true in connection with art. The word as applied to literature is not far from meaning intelligent enjoyment; it signifies not only apprehension but comprehension; it denotes not so much accumulation as assimilation; it is not so much acquirement as appreciation.

By the study of literature can be meant nothing pedantic, nothing formal, nothing artificial. I should like to call the subject of these talks "Experiencing Literature," if the verb could be received in the same sense as in the old-fashioned phrase "experiencing religion." That is what I mean. The study of literature is neither less nor more than experiencing literature, — the taking it to heart and the getting to its heart.

To most persons to study literature means nothing more than to read. There is, it is true, a vague general notion that it is the reading of some particular class of books, not always over clearly defined. It is not popularly supposed that the reading of an ordinary newspaper is part of the study of literature; while on the other hand there are few persons who can imagine that the perusal of Shakespeare, however casual, can be anything else. Since literary art is in the form of written works, reading is of course essential; but by study we mean something more grave and more fruitful than the mere surface acquaintance with books, no matter how high in the scale of excellence these may be.

The study of literature, in the true signification of the phrase, is that act by which the learner gets into the attitude of mind which enables him to enter into that creative thought which is the soul of every real book. It is easily possible, as every reader knows, to read without getting below the surface; to take a certain amount of intellectual account of that which we skim; to occupy with it the attention, and yet not to be at all in the mood which is indispensable for proper comprehension. It is this which makes it possible for the young girl of the present day to read novels which her more sophisticated brothers cannot look at without blushing to see them in her hands — at least, we hope that it is this! We all have moments when from mental weariness, indifference, indolence, or abstraction, we slide over the pages as a skater goes over the ice, never for a moment having so much as a glimpse of what is hidden beneath the surface. This is not the thing about which we are talking. We mean by study the making our own all that is contained in the books which we read; and not only all that is said, but still more all that is suggested; all that is to be learned, but above everything all that is to be felt.

The object of the study of literature is always a means and not an end, and yet in the development of the mind no means can fulfill its purpose which is not an enjoyment. Goethe has said: " Woe to that culture which points man always to an end, instead of making him happy by the way." No study is of any high value which is not a delight in itself; and equally, no study is of value which is pursued simply for itself. Every teacher knows how futile is work in which the pupil is not interested, — in other words, which is not a pleasure to him. The mind finds delight in all genuine activity and acquirement; and the student must take pleasure in his work or he is learning little. Some formal or superficial knowledge he may of course accumulate. The learning of the multiplication table is not to be set aside as useless because it is seldom accompanied by thrills of passionate enjoyment. There must be some drudgery in education; but at least what I have said certainly holds good in all that relates to the deeper and higher development of the mind.

The study of literature, then, is both a duty and a delight; a pleasure in itself and a help toward what is better. By it one approaches the comprehension of those books which are to be ranked as works of art. By it one endeavors to fit himself to enter into communication with the great minds and the great imaginations of mankind. What we gain in this may be broadly classified as pleasure, social culture, and a knowledge of life. Any one of these terms might almost be made to include the other two, but the division here is convenient in discussion.

Pleasure in its more obvious meaning is the most superficial, although the most evident, gain from art. In its simplest form this is mere amusement and recreation. We read, we say, "to pass the time." There are in life hours which need to be beguiled; times when we are unequal to the fatigue or the worry of original thought, or when some present reality is too painful to be faced. In these seasons we desire to be delivered from self, and the self-forgetfulness and the entertainment that we find in books are of unspeakable relief and value. This is of course a truism; but it was never before so insistently true as it is to-day. Life has become so busy, it is in a key so high, so nervously exhaustive, that the need of amusement, of recreation which shall be a relief from the severe nervous and mental strain, has become most pressing. The advance of science and civilization has involved mankind in a turmoil of multitudinous and absorbing interests from the pressure of which there seems to us no escape except in self-oblivion; and the most obvious use of reading is to minister to this end.

At the risk of being tedious it is necessary to remark in passing that herein lies a danger not to be passed over lightly. There is steadily increasing the tendency to treat literature as if it had no other function than to amuse. There is too much reading which is like opium-eating or dram-drinking. It is one thing to amuse one's self to live, and quite another to live to amuse one's self. It is universally conceded, I believe, that the intellect is higher than the body; and I cannot see why it does not follow that intellectual debauchery is more vicious than physical. Certainly it is difficult to see why the man who neglects his intellect while caring scrupulously for his body is on a higher moral plane than the man who, though he neglect or drug his body, does cultivate his mind.

In an entirely legitimate fashion, however, books may be read simply for amusement; and greatly is he to be pitied who is not able to lose himself in the enchantments of books. A physical cripple is hardly so sorrowful an object. Everybody knows the remark attributed to Talleyrand, who is said to have answered a man who boasted that he had never learned whist: "What a miserable old age you are preparing for yourself." A hundredfold is it true that he who does not early cultivate the habit of reading is neglecting to prepare a resource for the days when he shall be past active life. While one is in the strength of youth or manhood it is possible to fill the mind with interests of activity. As long as one is engaged in affairs directly the need of the solace of books is less evident and less pressing. It is difficult to think without profound pity of the aged man or woman shut off from all important participation in the work or the pleasure of the world, if the vicarious enjoyment of human interests through literature be also lacking. It is amazing how little this fact is realized or insisted upon. There is no lack of advice to the young to provide for the material comfort of their age, but it is to be doubted whether the counsel to prepare for their intellectual comfort is not the more important. Reading is the garden of joy to youth, but for age it is a house of refuge.

The second object which one may have in reading is that of social cultivation. It is hardly necessary to remark how large a part books play in modern conversation, or how much one may add to one's conversational resources by judicious reading. It is true that not a little of the modern talk about books is of a quality to make the genuine lover of literature mingle a smile with a sigh. It is the result not of reading literature, so much as of reading about literature. It is said that Boston culture is simply diluted extract of "Littell's Living Age;" and in the same spirit it might be asserted that much modern talk about books is the extract of newspaper condensations of prefaces. The tale is told of the thrifty paupers of a Scotch almshouse that the aristocrats among them who had friends to give them tea would steep and re-steep the precious herb, then dry the leaves, and sell them to the next grade of inmates. These in turn, after use, dried the much-boiled leaves once again, and sold them to the aged men to be ground up into a sort of false snuff with which the poor creatures managed to cheat into feeble semblance of joy their withered nostrils. I have in my time heard not a little so-called literary conversation which seemed to me to have gone to the last of these processes, and to be a very poor quality of thrice-steeped tea-leaf snuff! Indeed, it must be admitted that in general society book talk is often confined to chatter about books which had better not have been read, and to the retailing of second-hand opinions at that. The majority of mankind are as fond of getting their ideas as they do their household wares, at a bargain counter. It is perhaps better to do this than to go without ideas, but it is to be borne in mind that on the bargain counter one is sure to find only cheap or damaged wares.

Real talk about books, however, the expression of genuine opinions about real literature, is one of the most delightful of social pleasures. It is at once an enjoyment and a stimulus. From it one gets mental poise, clearness and readiness of ideas, and mental breadth. It is so important an element in human intercourse that it is difficult to conceive of an ideal friendship into which it does not enter. There have been happy marriages between men and women lacking in cultivation, but no marriage relation can be so harmonious that it may not be enriched by a community of literary tastes. A wise old gentleman whom I once knew had what he called an infallible receipt for happy marriages: "Mutual love, a sense of humor, and a liking for the same books." Certainly with these a good deal else might be overlooked. Personally I have much sympathy with the man who is said to have claimed a divorce on the ground that his wife did not like Shakespeare and would read Ouida. It is a serious trial to find the person with whom one must live intimately incapable of intellectual talk.

He who goes into general society at all is expected to be able to keep up at least the appearance of talking about literature with some degree of intelligence. This is an age in which the opportunities for what may be called cosmopolitan knowledge are so general that it has come to be the tacit claim of any society worth the name that such knowledge shall be possessed by all. I do not, of course, mean simply that acquaintance with foreign affairs which is to be obtained from the newspapers, even all wisdom as set forth in their vexingly voluminous Sunday editions. I mean that it is necessary to have with the thought of other countries, with their customs, and their habits of thought, that familiarity which is by most to be gained only by general reading. The multiplication of books and the modern habit of travel have made an acquaintance with the temper of different peoples a social necessity almost absolute.

To a great extent is it also true that modern society expects a knowledge of social conditions and æsthetic affairs in the past. This is not so much history, formally speaking, as it is the result of a certain familiarity with the ways, the habits of thought, the manners of bygone folk. Professor Barrett Wendell has an admirable phrase: "It is only in books that one can travel in time." What in the present state of society is expected from the accomplished man or woman is that he or she shall have traveled in time. He shall have gone back into the past in the same sense as far as temper of mind is concerned that one goes to Europe; shall have observed from the point of view not of the dry historian only, but from that of the student of humanity in the broadest sense. It is the humanness of dwellers in distant lands or in other times which most interests us; and it is with this that he who would shine in social converse must become familiar.

The position in which a man finds himself who in the company of educated men displays ignorance of what is important in the past is illustrated by a story told of Carlyle. At a dinner of the Royal Academy in London, Thackeray and Carlyle were guests, and at the table the talk among the artists around them turned upon Titian. "One fact about Titian," a painter said, "is his glorious coloring." "And his glorious drawing is another fact about Titian," put in a second. Then one added one thing in praise and another another, until Carlyle interrupted them, to say with egotistic emphasis and deliberation: "And here sit I, a man made in the image of God, who knows nothing about Titian, and who cares nothing about Titian; — and that's another fact about Titian." But Thackeray, who was sipping his claret and listening, paused and bowed gravely to his fellow-guest. "Pardon me," he said, "that is not a fact about Titian. It is a fact — and a very lamentable fact — about Thomas Carlyle." Attempts to carry off ignorance under the guise of indifference or superiority are common, but in the end nobody worth deceiving is misled by them,

It is somewhat trite to compare the companionship of good books to that of intellectual persons, and yet the constant repetition of a truth does not make it false. To know mankind and to know one's self are the great shaping forces which mould character. It has too often been said to need to be insisted upon at any great length that literature may largely represent experience; but it may fitly be added that in reading one is able to choose the experiences to which he will be exposed. In life we are often surrounded by what is base and ignoble, but this need not happen to us in the library unless by our deliberate choice. Emerson aptly says: —

Go with mean people and you think life is mean. Then read Plutarch, and the world is a proud place, peopled with men of positive quality, with heroes and demigods standing around us, who will not let us sleep.

It so often happens that we are compelled in daily life to encounter and to deal with mean people that our whole existence would be in great danger of becoming hopelessly sordid and mean were it not for the blessed company of great minds with whom we may hold closest communion through what they have written.

One more point in regard to the social influence of reading should be mentioned. Social ease and aplomb can of course be gained in no way save by actual experience; but apart from this there is nothing else so effective as familiarity with the best books. Sympathetic comprehension of literature is the experience of life taken vicariously. It is living through the consciousness of others, and those, moreover, who are the cleverest and most far-reaching minds of all time. The mere man of books brought into contact with the real world is confused and helpless; but when once the natural shyness and bewilderment have worn off, he is able to recall and to use the knowledge which he has acquired in the study, and rapidly adapts himself to any sphere that he may find himself in. I do not mean that a man may read himself into social grace and ease; but surely any given man is at a very tangible advantage in society for having learned from books what society is.

IV

WHY WE STUDY LITERATURE

In all that is said in the last chapter we have dealt only with the outward and accidental, barely touching upon the really significant and deeper meanings of our subject. The third object which I named, the gaining a knowledge of life, transcends all others.

The desire to fathom the meaning of life is the most constant and universal of human longings. It is practically impossible to conceive of consciousness separated from the wish to understand self and the significance of existence. This atom selfhood, sphered about by the infinite spaces of the universe, yearns to comprehend what and where it is. It sends its thought to the farthest star that watches the night, and thence speeds it down the unsounded void, to search unweariedly for the answer of the baffling, insistent riddle of life. Whatever man does or dreams, hopes or fears, loves or hates, suffers or enjoys, has behind it the eternal doubt, the question which man asks of the universe with passionate persistence, — the meaning of life.

Most of all does man seek aid in solving this absorbing mystery. Nothing else interests the human like the human. The slatternly women leaning out of tenement-house windows and gossiping across squalid courts talk of their neighbors. The wisest philosopher studies the acts and the thoughts of men. In the long range between these extremes there is every grade of intelligence and cultivation; and in each it is the doings, the thoughts, most of all the feelings, of mankind which elicit the keenest interest. The motto of the Latin playwright is in reality the motto of the race: "Nothing human is indifferent to me."

We are all intensely eager to know what are the possibilities of humanity. We seek knowledge of them as an heir questions searchingly concerning the extent of the inheritance which has fallen to him. Literature is the inventory of the heritage of humanity. Life is but a succession of emotions; and the earnest mind burns with desire to learn what emotions are within its possibilities. The discoverer of an unsuspected capability of receiving delight, the realization of an unknown sensation, even of pain, increases by so much the extent of the possessions of the human being to whom he imparts it. As explorers in a new country tell one another of the springs upon which they have chanced, of the fertile meadows one has found, of the sterile rocks or the luscious jungle, so men tell one another of their fresh findings in emotion. The knowledge of life — this is the passionate quest of the whole race of men.

All that most deeply concerns man, all that reaches most penetratingly to the roots of being, is recorded, so far as humanity has been able to give to it expression, in art. Of all art, literature is perhaps the most universally intelligible; or, if not that, it is at least the most positively intelligible. Our interest in life shows itself in a burning curiosity to know what goes on in the minds of our friends; to discover what others make out of existence, what they find in its possibilities, its limitations, its sorrows, and its delights. In varying degrees, according to individual temperament, we pass life in an endeavor to discover and to share the feelings of other human beings. We explain our feelings, our motives; we wonder whether they look to others as they do to us; we speculate whether others have found a way to get from life more than we get; and above all are we consciously or unconsciously eager to learn whether any other has contrived means of finding in life more vivid sensations, more vibrant emotions, more far-reaching feelings than those which we experience. It is in this insatiable curiosity that our deepest interest in literature lies.

Books explain us to ourselves. They reveal to us capabilities in our nature before unsuspected. They make intelligible the meaning and significance of mental experiences. There are books the constant rereading of which presents itself to an imaginative man as a sort of moral duty, so great is the illumination which they throw upon the inner being. I could name works which I personally cannot leave long neglected without a feeling of conscious guilt. It is of books of this nature that Emerson says that they

Take rank in our life with parents and lovers and passionate experiences, so medicinal, so stringent, so revolutionary, so authoritative, — books which are the work and the proof of faculties so comprehensive, so nearly equal to the world which they paint, that though one shuts them with meaner ones, he feels the exclusion from them to accuse his way of living. — *Books.*

There are probably none of us who have lived in vital relations to literature who cannot remember some book which has been an epoch in our lives. The times and the places when and where we read them stand out in memory as those of great mental crises. We recall the unforgettable night in which we sat until the cold gray dawn looked in at the window reading Lessing's "Nathan the Wise," the sunny slope where we experienced Madame de Gasparin's "Near and Heavenly Horizons," the winter twilight in the library when that most strenuous trumpet blast of all modern ethical poetry, "Childe Roland to the Dark Tower Came," first rang in the ears of the inner self. We all have these memories. There are books which must to us always be alive. They have spoken to us; we have heard their very voices; we know them in our heart of hearts.

That desire for sympathy which is universal is another strong incentive to acquaintance with literature. The savage who is less miserable in fear or in suffering if he find a fellow whose living presence saves him from the awful sense of being alone is unconsciously moved by this desire. The more fully the race is developed the more is this craving for human companionship and human appreciation conscious. We know how impossible it is ever completely to blend our consciousness for the smallest instant with that of any other human being. The nearest approach to this is the sharing with another some common feeling. There are blissful moments when some other is absorbed in the same emotion as that which we feel; when we seem to be one with the heart and the mind of another creature because the same strong passion sways us both. These are the mountain-tops of existence. These are the times which stand out in our remembrance as those in which life has touched in seeming the divine impossible.

It is of the greatest rarity, however, that we find, even in our closest friends, that comprehension and delicate sympathy for which we long. Indeed, such is human egotism that it is all but impossible for any one so far to abandon his own personality as to enter fully into the more delicate and intangible feelings of his fellow. A friend is another self, according to the proverb, but it is apt to be himself and not yourself. To find sympathy which comes from a knowledge that our inmost emotions are shared we turn to books. Especially is this true in bereavement and in sorrow. The touch of a human hand, the wistful look in the eye of the friend who longs to help, or the mere presence of some beautiful and responsive spirit, is the best solace where comfort is impossible; but even the tenderest human presence may jar, while in books there is a consolation and a tenderness unhampered by the baffling sense of a consciousness still outside of our own no matter how strenuously it longs to be in perfect unity. I knew once a mother who had lost her only child, and who used to sit for hours pressing to her heart Plutarch's divinely tender letter to his wife on the death of his own little one. It was almost as if she felt her baby again in her arms, and the leather covers of the book were stained with tears consecrated and saving. Who could count the number to whom "In Memoriam" has carried comfort when living friends had no message? The critical defects of that poem are not far to seek; but it would ill become us to forget how many grief-laden hearts it has reached and touched. The book which lessens the pain of humanity is in so far higher than criticism.

Josiah Quincy used in his old age to relate how his mother, left a young widow by the death of her husband within sight of the shores of America when on his return from a mission to England, found comfort in the soothing ministration of books:—

> She cultivated the memory of my father, even in my earliest childhood, by reading me passages from the poets, and obliging me to learn by heart and repeat such as were best adapted to her own circumstances and feelings. Among others the whole leave-taking of Hector and Andromache, in the sixth book of Pope's Homer, was one of her favorite lessons. . . . Her imagination, probably, found consolation in the repetition of lines which brought to mind and seemed to typify her own great bereavement.

> And think'st thou not how wretched we shall be, —
> A widow I, a helpless orphan he?

These lines, and the whole tenor of Andromache's address and circumstances, she identified with her own sufferings, which seemed relieved by the tears my repetition of them drew from her.

This comforting power of literature is one which need not perhaps have been enlarged upon so fully, but it is one which has to do with the most intimate and poignant relations of life.

It is largely in virtue of the sympathy which it is possible to feel for books that from them we not only receive a knowledge of the capacities of human emotion, but we are given actual emotional experience as well. For literature has a twofold office. It not only shows the possibilities of life, but it may make these possibilities realities. If art simply showed us what might be without aiding us further, it would be but a banquet of Tantalus. We must have the substance as well as the shadow. We are born not only with a craving to know what emotions are the birthright of man, but with an instinctive desire to enter into that inheritance. We wish to be all that it is possible for men to be. The small boy who burns to be a pirate or a policeman when he grows up, is moved by the idea that to men of these somewhat analogous callings come a richness of adventure and a fullness of sensation which are not to be found in ordinary lives. The lad does not reason this out, of course; but the instinctive desire for emotion speaks in him. We are born with the craving to know to the full the emotions of the race. It is to few of us in modern civilized life that circumstances permit a widely extended experience in actual mental sensations. The commonplace actualities of every-day life show plain and dull beside the almost infinite possibilities of existence. The realization of the contrast makes not a few mortals unhappy and dissatisfied; but those who are wiser accept life as it is, and turn to art for the gratification of the instinctive craving which is unsatisfied by outward reality.

It may be that fate has condemned us to the most humdrum of existences. We trade or we teach or are lawyers or housekeepers, doctors or nurses, or the curse of the gods has fallen upon us and we are condemned to the dreariness of a life of pleasure-seeking. We cannot of ourselves know the delights of the free outlaw's life under "the greene shaw,"—the chase of the deer, the twang of the bowstring, the song of the minstrel, the relish of venison pasty and humming nut-brown ale, are not for us in the flesh. If we go into the library, however, take down that volume with the cover of worn brown leather, and give up the imagination to the guidance of the author, all these things become possible to the inner sense. We become aware of the reek of the woodland fire, the smell of the venison roasting on spits of ash-wood, the chatter of deep manly voices, the cheery sound of the bugle-horn afar, the misty green light of the forest, the soft sinking feel of the moss upon which in imagination we have flung ourselves

WHY WE STUDY LITERATURE 53

down, while Will Scarlet teases Friar Tuck yonder, and Allan-a-Dale touches light wandering chords on his harp. — Ah, where are the four walls of the library, where is the dull round of cares and trifles which involve us day by day? We are in merry Sherwood with bold Robin Hood, and we know what there was felt and lived.

We cannot in outward experience know how a great and generous heart must feel, broken by ingratitude and unfaith, deceived and tortured through its noblest qualities, outraged in its highest love. The poet says to us: " Come with me; and through the power of the imagination, talisman more potent than the ring of Solomon, we will enter the heart of Othello, and with him suffer this agony. We will endure the torture, since behind it is the exquisite delight of appeasing that insatiable thirst for a share in human emotions. Or would you taste the passion of young and ardent hearts, their woe at parting, and their resolved devotion which death itself cannot abate? We will be one with Romeo and one with Juliet." Thus, if we will, we may go with him through the entire range of mortal joys and sorrows. We live with a fullness of living beside which, it may be, our ordinary existence is flat and pale. We find the real life, the life of the imagination; and we recognize that this is after all more vital than our concern over the price of stocks, our petty bother about the invitation to the Hightops' ball on the twenty-fourth, or the silly pang of brief jealousy which we experienced when we heard that Jack Scribbler's sonnet was to appear in the next number of the magazine which had just returned our own poem "with thanks." The littlenesses of the daily round slip out of sight before the nobility of the life possible in the imagination.

It is not necessary to multiply examples of the pleasures possible through the imagination. Every reader knows how varied and how enchanting they are. To enter into them is in so far to fulfill the possibilities of life. The knowledge which is obtained through books is not the same, it is true, as that which comes from actual doing and enduring. Perhaps if the imagination were sufficiently developed there would be little difference. There have been men who have been hardly able to distinguish between what they experienced in outward life and what belonged solely to the inner existence. Coleridge and Wordsworth and Keats made no great or sharply defined distinction between the things which were true in fact and those that were true in imagination. To Blake the events of life were those which he knew through imagination, while what happened in ordinary, every-day existence he regarded as the accidental and the nonessential.

It will probably be thought, however, that those who live most abundantly are not likely to feel the need of testing existence and tasting emotions through the medium of letters. The pirate, when decks are red and smoke of powder is in the air, is not likely to retire to his cabin for a session of quiet and delightful reading; the lover may peruse sentimental ballads or make them, but on the whole everything else is subordinate to the romance he is living. It is when his lady-love keeps him at a distance that he has time for verse; not when she graciously allows him near. It is told of Darwin that his absorption in science destroyed not only his love of Shakespeare but even his power of enjoying music. The actual interests of life were so vivid that the artistic sense was numbed. The imagination exhausted itself in exploring the unknown world of scientific knowledge. It is to be noted that boys who go deeply into college sports, especially if they are on the "teams," are likely to become so absorbed in the sporting excitement that literature appears to them flat and tame. The general rule is that he who lives in stimulating and absorbing realities is thereby likely to be inclined to care less for literature.

It is to be remembered, however, that individual experience is apt to be narrow, and that it may be positively trivial and still engross the mind. That one is completely given up to affairs does not necessarily prove these affairs to be noble. It is generally agreed, too, that the mind is more elastic which is reached and developed by literature; and that even the scientist is likely to do better work for having ennobled his perceptions by contact with the thoughts of master spirits. Before Darwin was able to advance so far in science as to have no room left for art, he had trained his faculties by the best literature. At least it is time enough to give up books when life has become so full of action as to leave no room for them. This happens to few, and even those of whom it is true cannot afford to do without literature as an agent in the development and shaping of character.

The good which we gain from the experiences of life we call insight. No man or woman ever loved without thereby gaining insight into what life really is. No man has stood smoke-stained and blood-spattered in the midst of battle, caught away out of self in an ecstasy of daring, without thereby learning hitherto undreamed-of possibilities in existence. Indeed this is true of the smallest incident. Character is the result of experience upon temperament, as ripple-marks are the result of the coming together of sand and wave. In life, however, we are generally more slow to learn the lessons from events than from books. The author of genius has the art so to arrange and present his truths as to impress them upon the reader. The impressions of events remain with us, but it is not easy for ordinary mortals so to realize their meaning and so to phrase it that it shall remain permanent and clear in the mind. The mental vision is clouded, moreover, by the personal element. We are seldom able to be perfectly frank with ourselves. Self is ever the apologist for self. Knowledge without self-honesty is as a torch without flame; yet of all the moral graces self-honesty is perhaps the most difficult to acquire. In its acquirement is literature of the highest value. A man can become acquainted with his spiritual face as with his bodily countenance only by its reflection. Literature is the mirror in which the soul learns to recognize its own lineaments.

Above all these personal reasons which make literature worthy of the serious attention of earnest men and women is the great fact that upon the proper development and the proper understanding of it depend largely the advancement and the wise ordering of civilization. Stevenson spoke words of wisdom when he said : —

One thing you can never make Philistine natures understand; one thing, which yet lies on the surface, remains as unseizable to their wits as a high flight of metaphysics, — namely, that the business of life is mainly carried on by the difficult art of literature, and according to a man's proficiency in that art shall be the freedom and fullness of his intercourse with other men.

In a fine passage in a little-known pamphlet, James Hannay touches upon the relation of literature to life and to the practical issues of society : —

A notion is abroad that that only is "practical" which can be measured or eaten. Show us its net result in marketable form, the people say, and we will recognize it! But what if there be something prior to all such "net results," something higher than it? For example, the writing of an old Hebrew Prophet was by no manner of means "practical" in his own times! The supply of figs to the Judean markets, the price of oil in the synagogue-lamps, did not fluctuate with the breath of those inspired songs! But in due time the prophet dies, stoned, perhaps, . . . and in the course of ages, his words do have a "practical" result by acting on the minds of nations. . . . In England what has not happened from the fact that the Bible was translated? We have seen the Puritans — we know what we owe to them — what the world owes to them! A dozen or two of earnest men two centuries ago were stirred to the depths of their souls by the visions of earnest men many centuries before that ; do you not see that the circumstance has its practical influence in the cotton-markets of America at this hour? — Quoted in Espinasse's *Literary Recollections*.

It is impossible to separate the influences of literature from the growth of society and of civilization. It is because of the reaching of the imagination into the unknown vast which incloses man that life is what it is. The order that is given to butcher or baker or candlestick-maker is modified by the fact that Homer and Dante and Shakespeare sang; that the prophets and the poets and the men of imagination of whatever time and race have made thought and feeling what they are. "The world of imagination," Blake wrote, "is the world of eternity." Whatever of permanent interest and value man has achieved he has reached through this divine faculty, and it is only when man learns to know and to enter the world of imagination that he comes into actual contact with the vital and the fundamental in human life. Easily abused, like all the best gifts of the gods, art remains the noblest and the most enduring power at work in civilization ; and literature is its most direct embodiment. To it we go when we would leave behind the sordid, the mean, and the belittling. When we would enter into our birthright, when we remember that instead of being mere creatures of the dust we are the heirs of the ages, then it is through books that we find and possess the treasures of the race.

V

FALSE METHODS

THE most common intellectual difficulty is not that of the lack of ideas, but that of vagueness of ideas. Most persons of moderately good education have plenty of thoughts such as they are, but there is a nebulous quality about these which renders them of little use in reasoning. This makes it necessary to define what is meant by the Study of Literature, as in the first place it was necessary to define literature itself. Many have a formless impression that it is something done with books, a sort of mysterious rite known only to the initiated, and probably a good deal like the mysteries of secret societies, — more of a theory than an actuality. Others, who are more confident of their powers of accurate thinking, have decided that the phrase is merely a high-sounding name for any reading which is not agreeable, but which is recommended by text-books. Some take it to be getting over all the books possible, good, bad, and indifferent; while still others suppose it to be reading about books or their authors. There are plenty of ideas as to what the study of literature is, but the very diversity of opinion proves that at least a great many of these must be erroneous.

FALSE METHODS

In the first place the study of literature is not the mere reading of books. Going on a sort of Cook's tour through literature, checking off on lists what one has read, may be amusing to simple souls, but beyond that it means little and effects little. As the question to be asked in regard to a tourist is how intelligently and how observantly he has traveled, so the first consideration in regard to a reader is how he reads.

The rage for swiftness which is so characteristic of this restless time has been extended to fashions of reading. By some sort of a vicious perversion, the old saw that he who runs may read seems to have been transposed to "He who reads must run." In other words there is too often an assumption that the intellectual distinction of an individual is to be estimated by the rapidity with which he is able to hurry through the volumes he handles. Intellectual assimilation takes time. The mind is not to be enriched as a coal barge is loaded. Whatever is precious in a cargo is taken carefully on board and carefully placed. Whatever is delicate and fine must be received delicately, and its place in the mind thoughtfully assigned.

One effect of the modern habit of swift and careless reading is seen in the impatience with which anything is regarded which is not to be taken in at a glance. The modern reader is apt to insist that a book shall be like a theatre-poster. He must be able to take it all in with a look as he goes past it on a wheel, and if he cannot he declares that it is obscure. W. M. Hunt said, with

62 THE STUDY OF LITERATURE

bitter wisdom: "As print grows cheap, thinkers grow scarce." The enormous increase of books has bred a race of readers who seem to feel that the object of reading is not to read but to have read; not to enjoy and assimilate, but to have turned over the greatest possible number of authors. This idea of the study of literature is as if one selected as the highest social ideal the afternoon tea, where the visitor is presented to numberless strangers and has an opportunity of conversing rationally with nobody.

A class of self-styled students of literature far more pernicious than even the record-breaking readers is that of the gossip-mongers. These are they who gratify an innate fondness of gossip and scandal under the pretext of seeking culture, and who feed an impertinent curiosity in the name of a noble pursuit. They read innumerable volumes filled with the more or less spicy details of authors; they perhaps visit the spots where the geniuses of the world lived and worked. They peruse eagerly every scrap of private letters, journals, and other personal matter which is available. For them are dragged to light all the imperfect manuscripts which famous novelists have forgotten to burn. For them was perpetrated the infamy of the publication of the correspondence of Keats with Miss Brawne; to them Mrs. Stowe appealed in her foul book about Byron, which should have been burned by the common hangman. It is they who buy the newspaper descriptions of the back bedroom of the popular novelist and the accounts of the misunderstanding between the poet and his washerwoman. They scent scandal as swine scent truffles, and degrade the noble name of literature by making it an excuse for their petty vulgarity.

The race is by no means a new one. Milton complained of it in the early days of the church, when, he says : —

With less fervency was studied what St. Paul or St. John had written than was listened to one that could say : " Here he taught, here he stood, this was his stature, and thus he went habited," and, " O happy this house that harbored him, and that cold stone whereon he rested, this village where he wrought a miracle."

Schopenhauer, too, has his indignant protest against this class : —

Petrarch's house in Arqua, Tasso's supposed prison in Ferrara, Shakespeare's house in Stratford, Goethe's house in Weimar, with its furniture, Kant's old hat, the autographs of great men, — these things are gaped at with interest and awe by many who have never read their works.

All this is of course a matter of personal vanity. Small souls pride themselves upon having these things, upon knowing intimate details of the lives of prominent persons. They endeavor thus to attach themselves to genius, as burrs cling to the mane of a lion. The imagination has nothing to do with it; there is in it no love of literature. It is vanity pure and simple, a common vulgar vanity which substitutes self-advertisement and gossipmongering for respect and appreciation. Who can have tolerance for the man whose proudest boast is that he was in a crowd presented to some poet whose books he never read; for the woman who claims attention on the ground that she has from her seamstress heard particulars of the domestic infelicities of a great novelist; or for the gossip of either sex who takes pride in knowing about famous folk trifles which are nobody's business but their own?

A good many text-books encourage this folly, and there are not a few writers who pass their useless days in grubbing in the dust-heaps of the past to discover the unessential and unmeaning incidents in the lives of bygone worthies. They put on airs of vast superiority over mortals who scorn their ways and words; they have only pitying contempt for readers who suppose that the works of an author are what the world should be concerned with instead of his grocery bills and the dust on his library table. Such meddlers have no more to do with literature than the spider on the eaves of kings' houses has to do with affairs of state.

It is not that all curiosity about famous men is unwholesome or impertinent. The desire to know about those whose work has touched us is natural and not necessarily objectionable. It is outside of the study of literature, save in so far as it now and then — less often, I believe, than is usually assumed — may help us to understand what an author has written; yet within proper limits it is to be indulged in, just as we all indulge now and then in harmless gossip concerning our fellows. It is almost sure to be a hindrance rather than a help in the study of literature if it goes much beyond the knowledge of those circumstances in the life of an author which have directly affected what he has written. There are few facts in literary history for which we have so great reason to be devoutly thankful as that so little is known concerning the life of the greatest of poets. We are able to read Shakespeare with little or no interruption in the way of detail about his private affairs, and for this every lover of Shakespeare's poetry should be grateful.

The study of literature, it must be recognized farther, is not the study of the history of literature. The development of what are termed "schools" of literature; the change in fashions of expression; the modifications in verse-forms and the growth and decay of this or that phase of popular taste in books, are all matters of interest in a way. They are not of great value, as a rule, yet they will often help the reader to a somewhat quicker appreciation of the force and intention of literary forms. It is necessary to have at least a general idea of the course of literary and intellectual growth through the centuries in order to appreciate and comprehend literature, — the point to be kept in mind being that this is a means and not in itself an end. It is necessary, for instance, for the student to toil painfully across the wastes of print produced in the eighteenth century, wherein there is little really great save the works of Fielding; and where the reader has to endure a host of tedious books in order properly to appreciate the manly tenderness of Steele, the boyishly spontaneous realism of Defoe, the kindly humanity of Goldsmith, and the frail, exquisite pipe of Collins. The rest of the eighteenth century authors most of us read chiefly as a part of the mechanics of education. We could hardly get on intelligently without a knowledge of the polished primness of Addison, genius of respectability; the vitriolic venom of Swift, genius of malignity; the spiteful perfection of Pope, genius of artificiality; or the interminable attitudinizing of Richardson, genius of sentimentality. These authors we read quite as much as helps in understanding others as for their own sake. We do not always have the courage to acknowledge it, but these men do not often touch our emotions, even though the page be that of Swift, so much the greatest of them. We examine the growth of the romantic spirit through the unpoetic days between the death of Dryden and the coming of Blake and Coleridge and Wordsworth; and from such examination of the history of literature we are better enabled to form standards for the actual estimate of literature itself.

There is a wide and essential difference between really entering into literature and reading what somebody else has been pleased to say of it, no matter how wise and appreciative this may be. Of course the genuine student has small sympathy with those demoralizing flippancies about books which are just now so common in the guise of smart essays upon authors or their works; those papers in which adroit literary hacks write about books as the things with which they have meddled most. The man who reads for himself and thinks for himself realizes that these essayists are the gypsy-moths of literature, living upon it and at the same time doing their best to destroy it; and that the reading of these petty imitations of criticism is about as intellectual as sitting down in the nursery to a game of " Authors."

Even the reading of good and valuable papers is not the study of literature in the best sense. There is much of profit in such admirable essays as those, for instance, of Lowell, of John Morley, or of Leslie Stephen. Excellent and often inspiring as these may be, however, it is not to be forgotten that as criticisms their worth lies chiefly in the incitement which they give to go to the fountain-head. The really fine essay upon a masterpiece is at its best an eloquent presentment of the delights and benefits which the essayist has received from the work of genius; it shows the possibilities and the worth within the reach of all. Criticisms are easily abused. We are misusing the most sympathetic interpretation when we receive it dogmatically. In so far as they make us see what is high and fine, they are of value; in so far as we depend upon the perceptions of the critic instead of our own, they are likely to be a hindrance. It is easier to think that we perceive than it is really to see; but it is well to remember that a man may be plastered from head to feet with the opinions of others, and yet have no more genuine ideas of his own than has a bill-board because it is covered with posters. Genuine emotion is born of genuine conviction. A reader is really touched by a work of art only as he enters into it and comprehends it sympathetically. Another may point the way, but he must travel it for himself. Reading an imaginative work is like wooing a maiden. Another may give the introduction, but for real acquaintance and all effective love-making the suitor must depend upon himself if he would be well sped. Critics may tell us what they admire, but the vital question is what we in all truth and sincerity admire and appreciate ourselves.

VI

METHODS OF STUDY

WE have spoken of what the study of literature is not, but negations do not define. It is necessary to look at the affirmative side of the matter. And first it is well to remark that what we are discussing is the examination of literature, — literature, that is, in the sense to which we have limited the term by definition: "The adequate expression of genuine emotion." It is not intended to include trash, whether that present itself as undisguised rubbish or whether it mask under high-sounding names of Symbolism, Impressionism, Realism, or any other affected nomenclature whatever. It has never been found necessary to excuse the existence of the masterpieces of literature by a labored literary theory or a catchpenny classification. It is generally safe to suspect the book which must be defended by a formula and the writers who insist that they are the founders of a school. There is but one school of art — the imaginative.

"But," it may be objected, "in an age when the books of the world are numbered by millions, when it is impossible for any reader to examine personally more than an insignificant portion even of those thrust upon his notice, how is the learner to judge what are worthy of his attention? To this it is to be answered that there are works enough universally approved to keep the readiest reader more than busy through the span of the longest human life. We shall have occasion later to speak of especial authors and of especial books. Here it is enough to say that certainly at the start the student must be content to accept the verdict of those who are capable of judging for him. Herein lies one of the chief benefits to be derived from critics and essayists. As the learner advances, he will find that as his taste and appreciation advance with them will develop an instinct of choice. In the end he should be able almost at a glance to judge rightly whether a book is worthy of attention. In the meanwhile he need not go astray if he follow the lead of trustworthy experts.

In accepting the opinions of others it is of course proper to use some caution, and above all things it is important to be guided by common sense. The market is full of quack mental as well as of quack physical nostrums. There is a large and enterprising body of publishers who seem persuaded that they have reduced all literature to a practical industrial basis by furnishing patent outsides for newspapers and patent insides for aspiring minds. In these days one becomes intellectual by prescription, and it is impossible to tell how soon will be advertised the device of inoculation against illiteracy. Common sense and a sense of humor save one from many dangers, and it is well to let both have full play.

I have spoken earlier in these talks of the pleasure of literary study. One fundamental principle in the selection of books is that it is idle to read what is not enjoyed. For special information one may read that which is not attractive save as it serves the purpose of the moment; but in all reading which is of permanent value for itself, enjoyment is a prime essential. Reading which is not a pleasure is a barren mistake. The first duty of the student toward literature and toward himself is the same,—enjoyment. Either take pleasure in a work of art or let it alone.

It is idle to force the mind to attend to works which it does not find pleasurable, and yet it is necessary to read books which are approved as the masterpieces of literature. Here is a seeming contradiction; but it must be remembered that it is possible to arouse the mind to interest. The books which are really worth attention will surely attract and hold if they are once properly approached and apprehended. If a mind is indolent, if it is able to enjoy only the marshmallows and chocolate caramels of literature, it is not to be fed solely on literary sweetmeats. Whatever is read should be enjoyed, but it by no means follows that whatever can be enjoyed should be read. It is possible to cultivate the habit of enjoying what is good, what is vital, as it is easy to sink into the stupid and slipshod way of caring for nothing which calls for mental exertion. It requires training and purpose. The love of the best in art is possessed as a gift of nature by only a few, and the rest of us must labor for it. The full appreciation of the work of a master-mind comes to no one without effort. The reward of the student of literature is great, but his labor also is great. Literature is not like an empty public square, which even a blind beggar may cross almost unconsciously. It more resembles an enchanted castle beset with spell-infested forests and ghoul-haunted mountains ; a place into which only that knight may enter who is willing to fight his way through dangers and difficulties manifold; yet a place, too, of infinite riches and joys beyond the imaginings of dull souls.

It is a popular fallacy that art is to be appreciated without especial education. Common feeling holds that the reader, like the poet, is born and not made. It is generally assumed that one is endowed by nature with an appreciation of art as one is born with a pug nose. The only element of truth in this is the fact that all human powers are modified by the personal equation. One is endowed at birth with perceptions fine and keen, while another lacks them ; but no matter what one's natural powers, there must be cultivation. This cultivation costs care, labor, and patience. It is, it is true, labor which is in itself delightful, and one might easily do worse than to follow it for itself without thought of other end ; but it is still labor, and labor strenuous and long enduring.

It is first necessary, then, to make an endeavor to become interested in whatever it has seemed worth while to read. The student should try earnestly to discover wherein others have found it good. Every reader is at liberty to like or to dislike even a masterpiece; but he is not in a position even to have an opinion of it until he appreciates why it has been admired. He must set himself to realize not what is bad in a book, but what is good. The common theory that the critical faculties are best developed by training the mind to detect shortcomings is as vicious as it is false. Any carper can find the faults in a great work; it is only the enlightened who can discover all its merits. It will seldom happen that a sincere effort to appreciate a good book will leave the reader uninterested. If it does, it is generally safe to conclude that the mind is not ready for this particular work. There must be degrees of development; and the same literature is not adapted to all stages. If you cannot honestly enjoy a thing you are from one cause or another in no condition to read it. Either the time is not ripe or it has no message for your especial temperament. To force yourself to read what does not please you is like forcing yourself to eat that for which you have no appetite. There may be some nourishment in one case as in the other, but there is far more likely to be indigestion.

An essential condition of profitable reading is that it shall be intelligent. The extent to which some persons can go on reading without having any clear idea of what they read is stupefyingly amazing! You may any day talk in society with persons who have gone through exhaustive courses of reading, yet who from them have no more got real ideas than a painted bee would get honey from a painted flower. Fortunately ordinary mortals are not so bad as this; but is there one of us who is not conscious of having tobogganed down many and many a page without pausing thoroughly to seize and master a single thought by the way?

It is well to make in the mind a sharp distinction between apprehending and comprehending. The difference is that between sighting and bagging your game. To run hastily along through a book, catching sight of the meaning of the author, getting a general notion of what he would convey, — casually apprehending his work, — is one thing; it is quite another to enter fully into the thoughts and emotions embodied, to make them yours by thorough appreciation, — in a word to comprehend. The trouble which Gibbon says he took to get the most out of what he read must strike ordinary readers with amazement: —

> After glancing my eye over the design and order of a new book, I suspended the perusal until I had finished the task of self-examination; till I had resolved in a solitary walk all that I knew or believed or had thought on the subject of the whole work or of some particular chapter; I was then qualified to discern how much the author added to my original stock; and if I was sometimes satisfied by the agreement, I was sometimes armed by the opposition, of our ideas.

It often happens that the average person does not read with sufficient deliberation even to apprehend what is plainly said. If there be a succession of particulars, for instance, it is only the exceptional reader who takes the time to comprehend fully each in turn. Suppose the passage to be the lines in the "Hymn before Sunrise in the Vale of Chamouni:"—

> Your strength, your speed, your fury, and your joy,
> Unceasing thunder, and eternal foam.

The ordinary student gets a general and probably a vague impression of cataracts, dashing down from the glacier-heaped hills; and that is the whole of it. A poet does not put in a succession of words like this merely to fill out his line. Coleridge in writing undoubtedly realized the torrent so fully in his imagination that it was as if he were beholding it. "What strength!" was his first thought. "What speed," was the next. "What fury; yet, too, what joy!" Then the ideas of that fury and that joy made it seem to him as if the noise of the waters was the voice in which these emotions were embodied, and as if the unceasing thunder were a sentient cry; while the eternal foam was the visible sign of the mighty passions of the "five wild torrents, fiercely glad."

In the dirge in "Cymbeline," Shakespeare writes:—

> Fear no more the frown o' the great,
> Thou art past the tyrant's stroke;
> Care no more to clothe and eat;
> To thee the reed is as the oak;
> The sceptre, learning, physic, must
> All follow this, and come to dust.

As you read, do you comprehend the exquisite propriety of the succession of the ideas? Death has removed Fidele from the possibility of misfortune; even the lords of the world can trouble no longer. Nay, more; it has done away with all need of care for the sordid details of every-day life, food and raiment. All that earth holds is now alike indifferent to the dead; the pale, wind-shaken reed is neither more nor less important than the steadfast and enduring oak. And to this, the thought runs on, must come even the mighty, the sceptred ones of earth. Not learning, which is mightier than temporal power, can save from this; not physic itself, of which the mission is to fight with death, can in the end escape the universal doom.

<blockquote>All follow this, and come to dust.</blockquote>

Hurried over as a catalogue, to take one example more, how dull is the following from Marlowe's "Jew of Malta;" but how sumptuous it becomes when the reader gloats over the name of each jewel as would do the Jew who is speaking:—

<blockquote>
The wealthy Moor, that in the eastern rocks
Without control can pick his riches up,
And in his house heap pearls like pebble-stones,
Receive them free, and sell them by the weight;
Bags of fiery opals, sapphires, amethysts,
Jacinths, hard topaz, grass-green emeralds,
Beauteous rubies, sparkling diamonds,
And seld-seen costly stones of so great price
As one of them indifferently rated,
And of a carat of this quantity,
May serve, in peril of calamity,
To ransom great kings from captivity.
</blockquote>

I have not much sympathy with the trick of reading into an author all sorts of far-fetched meanings of which he can never have dreamed; but, as it is only by observing these niceties of language that a writer is able to convey delicate shades of thought and feeling, so it is only by appreciation of them that the reader is able to grasp completely the intention which lies wrapped in the verbal form.

To read intelligibly, it is often necessary to know something of the conditions under which a thing was written. There are allusions to the history of the time or to contemporary events which would be meaningless to one ignorant of the world in which the author lived. To see any point to the fiery and misplaced passage in "Lycidas" in which Milton denounces the hireling priesthood and the ecclesiastic evils of his day, one must understand something of theological politics. We are aided in the comprehension of certain passages in the plays of Shakespeare by familiarity with the conditions of the Elizabethan stage and of the court intrigues. In so far it is sometimes an advantage to know the personal history of a writer, and the political and social details of his time. For the most part the portions which require elaborate explanation are not of permanent interest or at least not of great importance. The intelligent reader, however, will not wish to be tripped up by passages which he cannot understand, and will therefore be likely to inform himself at least sufficiently to clear up these.

Any reader, moreover, must to some extent know the life and customs of the people among whom a work is produced. To one who failed to appreciate wherein the daily existence of the ancient Greeks differed from that of moderns, Homer would hardly be intelligible. It would be idle to read Dante under the impression that the Italy of his time was that of to-day; or to undertake Chaucer without knowing, at least in a general way, how his England was other than that of our own time. The force of language at a given epoch, the allusions to contemporary events, the habits of thought and custom must be understood by him who would read comprehendingly.

When all is said there will still remain much that must depend upon individual experience. If one reads in Lowell : —

> And there the fount rises; . . .
> No dew-drop is stiller
> In its lupin-leaf setting
> Than this water moss-bounded;

one cannot have a clear and lively idea of what is meant who has not actually seen a furry lupin-leaf, held up like a green, hairy hand, with its dewdrop, round as a pearl. The context, of course, gives a general impression of what the poet intended, but unless experience has given the reader this bit of nature-lore, the color and vitality of the passage are greatly lessened. One of the priceless advantages to be gained from a habit of careful reading is the consciousness of the significance of small things, and in consequence the habit of observing them carefully. When we have read the bit just quoted, for instance, we are sure to perceive the beauty of the lupin-leaf with its dew-pearl if it come in our way. The attention becomes acute, and that which would otherwise pass unregarded becomes a source of pleasure. The most sure way to enrich life is to learn to appreciate trifles.

There is a word of warning which should here be spoken to the over-conscientious student. The desire of doing well may lead to overdoing. The student, in his anxiety to accomplish his full duty by separate words, often lets himself become absorbed in them. He drops unconsciously from the study of literature into the study of philology. There have been hundreds of painfully learned men who have employed the whole of their misguided lives in encumbering noble books with philological excrescences. I do not wish to speak disrespectfully of the indefatigable clan characterized by Cowper as

> Philologists, who chase
> A panting syllable through time and space;
> Start it at home, and hunt it in the dark,
> To Gaul, to Greece, and into Noah's ark.

These gentlemen are extremely useful in their way and place; but the study of philology is not the study of literature. It is at best one of its humble bond-slaves. A philologist may be minutely acquainted with every twig in the family-tree of each obsolete word in the entire range of Elizabethan literature, and yet be as darkly and as completely ignorant of that glorious world of poetry as the stokers in an ocean steamer are of the beauty of the sunset seen from the deck. It is often necessary to know the derivation of a term, and perhaps something of its history, in order to appreciate its force in a particular usage; but to go through a book merely to pick out examples for philologic research is like picking to pieces a mosaic to examine the separate bits of glass.

While, moreover, attention to the force and value of details is insisted upon, it must never be forgotten that the whole is of more value than any or all of its parts. The reader must strive to receive the effect of a book not only bit by bit, and page by page, and chapter by chapter, but as a book. There should be in the mind a complete and ample conception of it as a unit. It is not enough to appreciate the best passages individually. The work is not ours until it exists in the mind as a beautiful whole, as single and unbroken as one of those Japanese crystal globes which look like spheres of living water. He who knows the worth and beauty of passages is like an explorer. He is neither a conqueror nor a ruler of the territory he has seen until it is his in its entirety.

I believe that to comparatively few readers does it occur to make deliberate and conscious effort to realize works as wholes. The impression which a book leaves in the thought is of course in some sense a result of what the book is as a unit; but this is seldom sharply clear and vivid. The greatest works naturally give the most complete impression, and the power of producing an effect as a whole is one of the tests of art. The writer of genius is able so to choose what is significant, and so to arrange his material that the appreciative reader cannot fail to receive some one grand and dominating impression. It is hardly possible, for instance, for any intelligent person to fail to feel the cumulative passion of " King Lear." The calamities which come upon the old man connect themselves in the mind of the reader so closely with one central idea that it is rather difficult to escape from the dominant idea than difficult to find it. In " Hamlet," on the other hand, it is by no means easy to gain any complete and adequate grasp of the play as a unit without careful and intimate study. It is, moreover, not sure that one has gained a full conception of a work as a whole because one has an impression even so strong as that which must come to any receptive reader of " King Lear " or " Othello." To be profoundly touched by the story is possible without so fully holding the tragedy comprehendingly in the mind that its poignant meaning kindles the whole imagination. We have not assimilated that from which we have received merely fragmentary impressions. The appreciative reading of a really great book is a profound emotional experience. Individual portions and notable passages are at best but as incidents of which the real significance is to be perceived only in the light of the whole.

The power of grasping a work of art as a unit is one which should be deliberately cultivated. It is hardly likely to come unsought, even to the most imaginative. It must rest, in the first place, upon a reading of books as a whole. Whatever in any serious sense is worth reading once is worth rereading indefinitely. It is idle to hope to grasp a thing as a whole until one has become familiar with its parts. When once the details are clear in the mind, it is possible to read with a distinct and deliberate sense of the share that each passage bears in the entire purpose. It is necessary, and I may add that it is enchanting, to reread until the detached points gather themselves together in the inner consciousness as molecules in a solution gather themselves into a crystal. The delight of being able to realize what an author had in mind as a whole is like that of the traveler who at last, after long days of baffling mists which allowed but broken glimpses here and there, sees before him the whole of some noble mountain, stripped clean of clouds, standing sublime between earth and heaven.

Whatever effect a book has must depend largely upon the sympathy between the reader and the author. To read sympathetically is as fundamental a condition of good reading as is to read intelligently. It is well known how impossible it is to talk with a person who is unresponsive, who will not yield his own mood, and who does not share another's point of view. On the other hand, we have all tried to listen to speakers with whom it was not in our power to find ourselves in accord, and the result was merely unprofitable weariness. For the time being the reader must give himself up to the mood of the writer; he must follow his guidance, and receive not only his words but his suggestions with fullest acquiescence of perception, whatever be the differences of judgment. What Hawthorne has said of painting is equally applicable to literature: —

A picture, however admirable the painter's art, and wonderful his power, requires of the spectator a surrender of himself, in due proportion with the miracle which has been wrought. Let the canvas glow as it may, you must look with the eye of faith, or its highest excellence escapes you. There is always the necessity of helping out the painter's art with your own resources of sensibility and imagination. Not that these qualities shall really add anything to what the master has effected; but they must be put so entirely under his control and work along with him to such an extent that, in a different mood, when you are cold and critical instead of sympathetic, you will be apt to fancy that the loftier merits of the picture were of your own dreaming, not of his creating. Like all revelations of the better life, the adequate perception of a great work demands a gifted simplicity of vision. — *Marble Faun*, xxxvii.

Often it is difficult to find any meaning in what is written unless the reader has entered into the spirit in which it was composed. I seriously doubt, for instance, whether the ordinary person, coming upon the following catch of satyrs, by Ben Jonson, is able to find it much above the level of the melodies of Mother Goose: —

> "Buz," quoth the blue fly,
> "Hum," quoth the bee;
> Buz and hum they cry,
> And so do we.
> In his ear, in his nose,
> Thus, do you see?
> He ate the dormouse;
> Else it was he.

If you are not able to make much out of this, listen to what Leigh Hunt says of it:—

> It is impossible that anything could better express than this, either the wild and practical joking of the satyrs, or the action of the thing described, or the quaintness and fitness of the images, or the melody and even harmony, the intercourse, of the musical words, one with another. None but a boon companion, with a very musical ear, could have written it. — *A Jar of Honey.*

If the reader has the key to the mood in which this catch is written, if he has given himself up to the sportive spirit in which " rare old Ben " conceived it, it is possible to find in it the merit which Hunt points out; but without thus giving ourselves up to the leadership of the poet it is hardly possible to make of it anything at all. The example is of course somewhat extreme, but the principle is universal.

It is always well in a first reading to give one's self up to the sweep of the work; to go forward without bothering over slight errors or small details. Notes are not for the first or the second perusal so much as for the third and so on to the hundredth. Dr. Johnson is right when he says:—

> Notes are often necessary, but they are necessary evils. Let him that is yet unacquainted with the powers of Shakespeare, and who desires to feel the highest pleasures that the drama can give, read every play from the first scene to the last, with utter negligence of all his commentators. When his fancy is once on the wing, let it not stoop to correction or explanation.

One of the great obstacles to the enjoyment of

any art is the too conscientious desire to enjoy. We are constantly hindered by the conventional responsibility to experience over each classic the proper emotion. The student is often so occupied in painful struggles to feel that which he has been told to feel that he remains utterly cold and unmoved. It is like going to some historic locality of noble suggestion, where an officious guide moves the visitor from one precious spot to another, saying in effect: "Here such an event happened. Now thrill. Sixpence a thrill, please." For myself, being of a somewhat contumacious character, I have never been able to thrill to order, even if a shilling instead of sixpence were the price of the luxury; and in the same way I am unable to follow out a prescribed set of emotions at the command of a text-book on literature. Perhaps my temperament has made me unjustly skeptical, but I have never been able to have much faith in the genuineness of feelings carried on at the ordering of an emotional programme. The student should let himself go. On the first reading, at least, let what will happen so you are swept along in full enjoyment. It is better to read with delight and misunderstand, than to plod forward in wise stupidity, understanding all and comprehending nothing; gaining the letter and failing utterly to achieve the spirit. The letter may be attended to at any time; make sure first of the spirit. I do not mean that one is to read carelessly; but I do mean that one is to read enthusiastically, joyously, and, if it be possible, even passionately.

The best test of the completeness with which one has entered into the heart of a book is just this keenness of enjoyment. Fully to share the mood of the author is to share something of the delight of creation. It is as if in the mind of the reader this work of beauty and of immortal significance was springing into being. This enjoyment, moreover, increases with familiarity. If you find that you do not care to take up again a masterpiece because you have read it once, you may pretty safely conclude that you have never truly read it at all. You have been over it, it may be, and gratified some superficial curiosity; but you have never got to its heart. Does one claim to be won to the heart of a friend and yet to be willing never to see that friend more?

One may, of course, outgrow even a masterpiece. There are authors who are genuine so far as they go, who may be enjoyed at one stage of growth, yet who as the student advances become insufficient and unattractive. The man who does not outgrow is not growing. One does not healthily tire of a real book, however, until he has become greater than that book. The interest which becomes weary of a masterpiece is more than half curiosity, and at best is no more than intellectual. It is not imaginative. Margaret Fuller confessed that she tired of everything she read, even of Shakespeare. She thereby unconsciously discovered the quality of mind which prevented her from being a great woman instead of merely a brilliant one. She fed her intellect upon literature; but she failed because literature does not reach to its highest function unless its appeal to the intellect is the means of touching and arousing the imagination; because the end of all art is not the mind but the emotions.

It may seem that enough has already been required to make reading the most serious of undertakings; yet there is still one requirement more which is of the utmost importance. He is unworthy to share the delights of great work who is not able to respect it; he has no right to meddle with the best of literature who is not prepared to approach it with some reverence. In the greatest books the master minds of the race have graciously bidden their fellows into their high company. The honor should be treated according to its worth. Irreverence is the deformity of a diseased mind. The man who cannot revere what is noble is innately degraded. When writers of genius have given us their best thoughts, their deepest imaginings, their noblest emotions, it is for us to receive them with bared heads. He is greatly to be pitied who, in reading high imaginative work, has never been conscious of a sense of being in a fine and noble presence, of having been admitted into a place which should not be profaned. Only that soul is great which can appreciate greatness. Remember that there is no surer measure of what you are than the extent to which you are able to rise to the heights of supreme books; the extent to which you are able to comprehend, to delight in, and to revere, the masterpieces of literature.

VII

THE LANGUAGE OF LITERATURE

WHATEVER intelligence man imparts to man, at least all beyond the crudest rudimentary beginnings, must be conveyed by conventions. There must have been an agreement, tacit or explicit, that a certain sign shall stand for a certain idea; and when that idea is to be expressed, this sign must be used. In order that the meaning of any communication may be understood, it is essential that the means of expression be appreciated by hearer as well as by speaker. We have agreed that in English a given sound shall represent a given idea; and to one who knows this tongue the specified sound, either spoken or suggested by letters, calls that idea up. To one unacquainted with English, the sound is meaningless, because he is not a party to the agreement which has fixed for it a conventional significance; or it may awake in his thought an idea entirely different, because he belongs to a nation where tacit agreement has fixed upon another meaning. The word " dot," for instance, has by English-speaking folk been appropriated to the notion of a trifling point or mark; while those who speak French, writing and pronouncing the word in the same way, take it to indicate a dowry.

In order to communicate with any man, it is necessary to know what is the set of conventions with which he is accustomed to convey and to receive ideas.

The principle holds also in art. There is a conventional language in sound or color or form as there is in words. It is broader as a rule, because oftener founded upon general human characteristics, because more directly and obviously borrowed from nature, and because not so warped and distorted by those concessions to utility which have modified the common tongues of men. Indeed, it might at first thought seem that the language of art is universal, but a little reflection will show that this is not the case. The sculpture of the Aztecs, for instance, is in an art language utterly different from that of the sculpture of the Greeks. If you recall the elaborately intricate uncouthness of the gods of old Yucatan, you will easily appreciate that the artists who shaped these did not employ the same artistic conventions as did the sculptors who breathed life into the Venus of Melos, or who embodied divine serenity and beauty in the Elgin marbles. To the Greeks those twisted and thick-lipped Aztec deities, clutching one another by their crests of plumes, or grasping rudely at one another's arms, would have conveyed no sentiment of beauty or of reverence; while it is equally to be supposed that the Aztec would have remained hardly moved before the wonders of Greek sculpture. The Hellenic art conventions, it is true, were more directly founded upon nature, and therefore more readily understood; but even this would not have overcome the fact that one nation had one art language and the other another. Those of you who were at the Columbian Exposition will remember how the music in the Midway Plaisance illustrated this same point. The weird strain of one or another savage or barbaric folk came to the ear with a strangeness which showed how ignorant we are of the language of the music of these dwellers in far lands. To us it was bizarre or moving, but we could form little idea how it struck the hearers to whom it was native and familiar. It was even all but impossible to know whether a given strain was felt by the savage performers to be grave or gay. Of all the varieties of sound which there surprised the ear, that evolved by the Chinese appeared most harsh and unmelodious. The almond-eyed Celestial seemed to delight in a concatenation of crash and caterwauling, mingled in one infernal cacophony at which the nerves tingled and the hair stood on end. Yet it is on record that when in the early days of European intercourse with China, the French missionary Amiot played airs by Rossini and Boieldieu to a Chinese mandarin of intelligence and of cultivation according to eastern standards, the Oriental shook his head disapprovingly. He politely expressed his thanks for the entertainment, but when pressed to give an opinion of the music he was forced to reply: "It is sadly devoid of meaning and expression, while Chinese music penetrates the soul." After we have smiled at the absurdity, from our point of view, of the penetration of the soul by Chinese music, we reflect that after all our music is probably as absurd to them as theirs to us. We perhaps recall the fact that even the cultivated Japanese, with their sensitive feeling for art, and their readiness to adopt occidental customs, complain of the effect of dividing music into regular bars, and making it, as they say, "chip-chop, chip-chop, chip-chop." The fact is that every civilization makes its art language as it makes its word language; and he who would understand the message must understand the conventions by which it is expressed.

We are apt to forget this fact of the conventionality of all language. We become so accustomed both to the speech of ordinary intercourse and to that of familiar art, that we inevitably come to regard them as natural and almost universal. No language, however, is natural, unless it be fair to apply that word to the most primitive signs of savages. It is an arbitrary thing, and as such it must be learned. We acquire the ordinary tongue of our race almost unconsciously, and while we are too young to reason about it. We gain the language of art later and more deliberately, although of course we may owe much to our early surroundings in this as in every other respect. The point to be kept in mind is that we do learn it; that it is not the gift of nature. This is of course true of all art; but here our concern is only with the fact that literature has as truly its own peculiar language as music or painting or sculpture, — its language, that is, distinct from the language of ordinary daily or common speech.

The conventions which serve efficiently to convey ordinary ideas and matter-of-fact statements, are not sufficient for the expression of emotions. The man who has to tell the price of pigs and potatoes, the amount of coal consumed in a locomotive engine, or the effect of political complications upon the stock-market, is able to serve himself sufficiently well with ordinary language. The novelist who has to tell of the bewitchingly willful worldliness of Beatrix Esmond, of the fateful and tragic experiences of Donatello and Miriam, the splendidly real impossibilities of the career of D'Artagnan and his three friends, the passion of Richard Feverel for Lucy, of Kmita for Olenka, of Marius for Cosette; the dramatist who endeavors to make his readers share the emotions of Lear and Cordelia, of Caliban and Desdemona, of Viola and Juliet; the poet who would picture the emotions of Pompilia, of Lancelot and Guinevere, of Porphyrio and Madeline, of Prometheus and Asia, — all these require an especial language.

The conveying from mind to mind of emotion is a delicate task. It is not difficult to make a man understand the price of oysters, but endeavor to share with a fellow-being the secrets of a moment of transcendent feeling, and you have an undertaking so complex, and so all but impossible, that if you can perfectly succeed in it you may justly call yourself the first writer of your age. This is the making of the intangible tangible; the highest

THE LANGUAGE OF LITERATURE 93

creative act of the imagination. The cleverness and the skill of man have been exhausted in devising means to impart to readers the thought and feeling, the passion and emotion, which sway the hearts of mankind. It is not necessary here to go into those devices which belong especially to the domain of rhetoric, — the mechanics of style. They are designated in the old-fashioned text-books by tongue-twisting Greek names which most of us have learned, and which all of us have forgotten. It is not with them that I am here concerned. They are meant to affect the reader unconsciously. It is with those matters which appeal to the conscious understanding that we have now to do; the conventions which are the language of literature as Latin was the language of Cæsar or Greek the tongue of Pericles.

I have spoken already of the necessity of understanding what is said in literature; this is, however, by no means the whole of the matter. It is of even greater importance to be clearly aware of what is implied. We test the imaginative quality of what is written by its power of suggestion. The writer who has imagination will have so much to say that he is forced to make a phrase call up a whole train of thought, a word bring vividly to the mind of the reader a picture or a history. This is what critics mean when they speak of the marvelous condensation of Shakespeare; and in either prose or verse the criterion of imaginative writing is whether it is suggestive. Imagination is the realizing faculty. It is the power of receiving as true the ideal. It is the accepting as actual that which is conjured up by the inner vision; the making vital, palpitant, and present that which is known to be materially but a dream. That which is written when the poet sees the unseen palpably before his inner eye is so filled with the vitality and actuality of his vision that it fills the mind of the reader as a tenth wave floods and overflows a hollow in the rocks of the shore. When Keats says of the song of the nightingale that it is

> The same that oft-times hath
> Charm'd magic casements, opening on the foam
> Of perilous seas in faery lands forlorn,

all the romance and witchery of faery-lore are in this single phrase. The reader feels the glow of delight, the fascination of old tales which have pleased mankind from the childhood of the race. Into two lines the poet has condensed the fragrance of a thousand flowers of folk-lore.

In the best literature what is said directly is often of less importance than what is meant but not said. In dealing with imaginative writers, it is necessary to keep always in mind the fact that the literal meaning is but a part, and often not the greater part. The implied, the indirect, is apt to be that for the sake of which the work is written.

In its earlier stages all language is largely made up of comparisons. The fact that every tongue is full of fossil similes has been constantly commented upon, and this fact serves to illustrate how greatly the force of a word may be diminished if its original meaning is lost sight of. If, in ordinary conversation, to take a common illustration, some old-fashioned body now speak of a clergyman as a "pastor," it is to be feared that the word connotes little, unless it be a suspicion of rustic seediness in apparel, a certain provincial narrowness, and perhaps a conventional piety. When the word was still in its prime, it carried with it the force of its derivation; it spoke eloquently of one who ministered spiritual food to his followers, as a shepherd ministers to his flock. A pastor may now be as good as a pastor was then, but the title has ceased to do him justice. The freshness and force of words get worn off in time, as does by much use the sharpness of outline of a coin. We need constantly to guard against this tendency of language. We speak commonly enough in casual conversation of "a sardonic smile," but the idea conveyed is no more than that of a forced and heartless grin. As far back as the days of Homer, some imaginative man compared the artificial and sinister smile of a cynic to the distortions and convulsions produced by a poisonous herb in Sardinia; and from its very persistence we may fancy how forcible and striking was the comparison in its freshness. Of course, modern writers do not necessarily keep in mind the derivation of every word and phrase which they employ; but they do at least use terms with so much care for propriety and exactness that it is impossible to seize the whole of their meaning, unless we appreciate the niceties of their language. Ruskin says rightly: —

You must get yourself into the habit of looking intensely at words, and assuring yourself of their meaning, syllable by syllable, letter by letter. . . . You might read all the books in the British Museum (if you could live long enough), and remain an utterly "illiterate," uneducated person; but if you read ten pages of a good book, letter by letter,— that is to say, with real accuracy, — you are forevermore in some measure an educated person. — *Of Kings' Treasuries.*

Unless our attention has been especially called to the fact, there are few of us who at all realize how carelessly it is possible to read. We begin in the nursery to let words pass without attaching to them any idea which is really clear. We nourish our infant imaginations upon Mother Goose, and are content to go all our days in ignorance even of the meaning of a good many of the words so fondly familiar in pinafore days. We are all acquainted with the true and thrilling tale how

> Thomas T. Tattamus took two tees
> To tie two tups up to two tall trees;

but how many of us know what either a "tee" or a "tup" is? We have all been stirred in our susceptible youth by the rhyme wherein is recounted the exciting adventure of the four and twenty tailors who set forth to slay a snail, but who retreated in precipitate confusion when

> She put out her horns like a little Kyloe cow;

but it is to be feared that the proportion of us is not large who have taken the trouble to ascertain what is a Kyloe cow. Or take the well-worn ditty : —

> Cross-patch,
> Draw the latch,
> Sit by the fire and spin.

Have you ever stopped to reflect that "draw the latch" means to pull in the latch-string, and that in the days of homely general hospitality to which this contrivance belonged the image presented by the verse was that of a misanthropic hag, shutting herself off from her neighbors and sulking viciously by her fire behind a door rudely insulting the caller with the empty hole of the latch-string?

Perhaps this seems trifling; and it may easily be insisted that these rhymes become familiar to us while we are still too young to think of the exact meaning of anything. The question then is whether we do better when we are older. We are accustomed, very likely, to hear in common speech the phrase "pay through the nose." Do you know what that means, or that it goes back to the days of the Druids? When you hear the phrase "where the shoe pinches" do you recall Plutarch's story? Does the anecdote of St. Ambrose come to mind when the saying is "At Rome do as the Romans do"? It happens every few years that the newspapers are full of more or less excited talk about a "gerrymander." Does the word bring before the inner eye that uncouth monster wherewith the caricaturist of his day vexed the soul of Governor Gerry? I have tried to select examples which are not remote from the talk of every day. It seems to me that these illustrate well enough how apt we are to accept words and phrases as we accept a silver dollar, with very little idea of the intrinsic worth of what we are getting. This may be made to do well enough in practical buying and selling, but it is eminently unsatisfactory in matters intellectual or æsthetic. In the study of literature approximations are apt to be pretty nearly worthless.

The most obvious characteristic in literary language is that of allusion. Constantly does the reader of imaginative works encounter allusions to the Bible, to mythology, to history, to folk-lore, and to literature itself. To comprehend an author it is needful to realize fully what he had in mind when using these. They are the symbols of thoughts and feelings which are not to be expressed in ordinary ways. When we are familiar with the matter alluded to we see by the sudden and vivid light which is cast over the page by the comparison or the suggestion how expressive and comprehensive this form of language may be. To the reader who is ignorant the allusion is of course a stumbling-block and a rock of offense. It is like a sentence in an unknown tongue, which not only conceals its meaning but gives one an irritated sense of being shut out of the author's counsels.

It is probable that in English literature the allusions to the Bible are more numerous than any other. We shall have occasion later to speak of the place and influence of the King James version upon the literature of our tongue, and here we have to do only with those cases in which a scriptural reference is made part of the special language of an author. Again and again it happens that a writer takes advantage of the associations which cluster about a phrase or an incident of the Bible, and by a simple touch brings up in the mind of the understanding reader all the sentiments connected with the original.

With many of the more common of these phrases it is impossible for any one who associates with educated persons not to be familiar. They have become part and parcel of the common speech of the time. We speak of the "widow's mite," of a "Judas' kiss," of "the flesh-pots of Egypt," of "a still, small voice," of a "Jehu," a "perfect Babel," a "Nimrod," of "bread upon the waters," and of a "Delilah." The phrases have to a considerable extent acquired their own meaning, so that even one who is not familiar with the Scriptures is not likely to have difficulty in getting from them a general idea. To the reader who is acquainted with the force and origin of these terms, however, they have a vigor and significance which for others they must lack. The name Jehu brings up to him not merely a driver on a New England stage-coach, but the figure of the newly crowned usurper rushing down to the slaughter of King Joram, his master, when the watchman upon the wall looked out and said: "The driving is like the driving of Jehu, the son of Nimshi; for he driveth furiously." The phrase "bread upon the waters" affords a good illustration here. Perhaps most readers are likely to know the origin of the quotation, and probably the promise which concludes it. The number is smaller who realize the figure to be that of the oriental farmer casting abroad the seed-rice over flooded fields, sowing for the harvest which he shall find "after many days." The phrase "a still, small voice" has become dulled by common use, — one might almost say profane, since the quotation is of a quality which should render it too dignified and noble for careless employment. It speaks to the reader who knows its origin of that magnificently impressive scene on Horeb when Elijah stood on the mount before the Lord: —

And behold, the Lord passed by, and a great and strong wind rent the mountain, and brake in pieces the rocks before the Lord; but the Lord was not in the wind: and after the wind an earthquake; but the Lord was not in the earthquake: and after the earthquake a fire; but the Lord was not in the fire: and after the fire a still, small voice. And it was so, when Elijah heard it, that he wrapped his face in his mantle, and went out and stood in the entering in of the cave. And behold, there came a voice unto him, and said: " What doest thou here, Elijah? "— 1 *Kings* xix. 11–13.

It is not necessary to dwell upon this class of allusions. The reader who expects to get from them their full force must know the original; and while in ordinary speech these phrases are used carelessly and with little regard for their full significance, they are in the work of imaginative writers to be taken for all that they can and should convey.

There are other Biblical allusions which are less common and less obvious. When in the " Ode on the Nativity," Milton speaks of

—— that twice batter'd god of Palestine,

the verse means much to the reader who recalls the double fall of the fish-tailed god Dagon before the captured ark of Israel, but to others it is likely to mean nothing whatever. To be ignorant of the tale of Shadrach, Meshach, and Abed-nego is to miss completely the force of Hazlitt's remark that certain artists are so absorbed in their own productions that "they walked through collections of the finest works like the Children in the Fiery Furnace, untouched, unapproached." Not to know the declaration of St. Paul of what he had suffered for his faith[1] is to lose the point of Tennyson's verse

> Not in vain,
> Like Paul with beasts, I fought with death.

Prose and poetry are alike full of scriptural phraseology. In short, for the understanding of the language of allusion in English literature a knowledge of the English Bible is neither more nor less than essential.

Another class of allusions frequent in literature is the mythological. Here also we find phrases which have passed so completely into every-day currency that we hear and use them almost without reflecting upon their origin. "Scylla and Charybdis," "dark as Erebus," "hydra-headed," and "Pandora's box," are familiar examples. We speak of "a herculean task" without in the least calling to mind the labors of Hercules, and employ the phrase "the thread of life" without seeming

[1] If after the manner of men I have fought with beasts at Ephesus, what advantageth it me, if the dead rise not?—1 *Cor.* xv. 32.

to see the three grisly Fates, spinning in the chill gray dusk of their cave. We have gone so far as to condense a whole legend into a single word, and then to ignore the story. We say " lethean," " mercurial," " aurora," and " bacchanalian," without recalling their real significance. It is obvious how a perception of the original meaning of these terms must impart vividness to their use or to their understanding. There are innumerable instances, more particular, in which it is essential to know the force of a reference to old myths, lest the finer meaning of the author be altogether missed. In " The Wind-Harp " Lowell wrote: —

> I treasure in secret some long, fine hair
> Of tenderest brown . . .
> I twisted this magic in gossamer strings
> Over a wind-harp's Delphian hollow.

In the phrase " a wind-harp's Delphian hollow" the poet has suggested all the mysterious and fateful utterances of the abyss from which the Delphic priestess sucked up prophecies, and he has prepared the comprehending reader for the oracular murmur which swells from the instrument upon which have been stretched chords twisted from the hair of the dead loved one. To miss this suggestion is to lose a vital part of the poem. When Keats writes of " valley-lilies whiter still than Leda's love," unless there come instantly to the mind the image of the snowy swan whose form Jove took to win Leda, the phrase means nothing. The woeful cry in " Antony and Cleopatra,"

> The shirt of Nessus is upon me ; teach me,
> Alcides, thou mine ancestor, thy rage,

is full of keen-edged horror when one recalls the garment poisoned with his own blood by which the centaur avenged himself on Hercules. In a flash it brings up the picture of the demigod tearing his flesh in more than mortal agony, and calling to Philoctetes to light the funeral pyre that he might be consumed alive. It is not needful to multiply examples since they so frequently present themselves to the reader. The only point to be made is that here we have another well defined division of literary language.

Allusion to history is another characteristic form of the language of literature. References to classic story are perhaps more common than those to general or modern, but both are plentiful. Sometimes the form is that of a familiar phrase, as "a Cadmean victory," "a Procrustean bed," "a crusade," "a Waterloo," and so on. Phrases like these are easily understood, although it is hardly possible to get their full effect without a knowledge of their origin. What, however, would this passage in Gray's "Elegy" convey to one unfamiliar with English history? —

> Some village Hampden, that with dauntless breast
>   The little tyrant of his fields withstood;
> Some mute, inglorious Milton here may rest;
>   Some Cromwell, guiltless of his country's blood.

It is necessary to know about the majestic figure of ivory and gold which the Athenian sculptor wrought, or one misses the meaning of Emerson's couplet, —

> Not from a vain or shallow thought
> His awful Jove young Phidias brought.

Shakespeare abounds in examples of this use of allusions to history to produce a clear or vivid impression of some emotion or thought.

> I will make a Star-chamber matter of it.
> *Merry Wives*, i. 1.
>
> Though Nestor swear the jest be laughable.
> *Merchant of Venice*, i. 1.
>
> Even such a man, so faint, so spiritless,
> So dull, so dead in look, so woe-begone,
> Drew Priam's curtain in the dead of night,
> And would have told him half his Troy was burnt.
> 2 *Henry IV.*, i. 1.

The reader must know something of the Star-chamber, of the gravity and wisdom of Nestor, of the circumstances of the tragic destruction of Troy, or these passages can have little meaning for him.

Sometimes references of this class are less evident, as where Byron speaks of

> The starry Galileo with his woes;

or where Poe finely compresses the whole splendid story of antiquity into a couple of lines: —

> To the glory that was Greece
> And the grandeur that was Rome.

If we have in mind the varied and inspiring story of Greece and Rome, these lines unroll before us like a matchless panorama. We linger over them to let the imagination realize the full richness of their suggestion. The heart beats more quickly, and we find ourselves murmuring over and over to ourselves with a kindling sense of warmth and glow: —

> To the glory that was Greece
> And the grandeur that was Rome.

Poe affords an excellent example of this device of historical allusion carried to its extreme. In "The Fall of the House of Usher," there is a stanza which reads: —

> Wanderers in that happy valley
>   Through two luminous windows saw
> Spirits moving musically
>   To a lute's well-tunèd law,
> Round about a throne, where sitting
>   (Porphyrogene!)
> In state his glory well-befitting,
>   The ruler of the realm was seen.

If the reader chance to know that in the great palace of Constantine the Great at Constantinople there was a building of red porphyry, which by special decree was made sacred to motherhood, and that here the princes of the blood were born, being in recognition called "porphyrogene," there will come to him the vision which Poe desired to evoke. The word will suggest the regal splendors of the Byzantine court at a time when the whole world babbled of its glories, and will give to the verse a richness of atmosphere which could hardly be produced by any piling up of specific details. The reader who is not in possession of this information can only stumble over the word as I did in my youth, with an aggrieved feeling of being shut out from the inner mysteries of the poem. I spoke of this as an extreme instance of the use of this form of literary language, because the knowledge needed to render it intelligible is more unusual and special than that generally appealed to by writers. It is one of those bold strokes which are tremendously effective when they succeed, but which are likely to fail with the ordinary reader.

After historic allusion comes that to folk-lore, which used to be a good deal appealed to by imaginative writers. Some knowledge of old beliefs is often essential to the comprehension of earlier authors. Suckling, for instance, says very charmingly : —

> But oh, she dances such a way!
> No sun upon an Easter day
> Is half so fine a sight!

The reference, of course, is to the superstition that the sun on Easter morning danced for joy at the coming of the day when the Lord arose. To get the force of the passage, it is necessary to put one's self into the mood of those who believed this pretty legend. In the same way it is only to one who is acquainted with the myth of the lubber fiend, the spirit who did the work of the farm at night for the wage of a bowl of cream set for him beside the kitchen fire, that there is meaning in the lines in "L'Allegro : " —

> Tells how the grudging goblin sweat
> To earn his cream-bowl duly set,
> When in one night, ere glimpse of morn,
> His shadowy flail hath thresh'd the corn
> That ten day-laborers could not end ;
> And, stretch'd out all the chimney's length,
> Basks at the fire his hairy strength ;
> And crop-full out of doors he flings,
> Ere the first cock his matin rings.

There is much of this folk-lore language in Shakespeare, and in our own time Browning has perhaps more of it than any other prominent author. It may be remarked in passing, that Browning, who loved odd books and read a good many strange old works which are not within general reach, is more difficult in this matter of allusion than any other contemporary. References of this class are generally a trouble to the ordinary reader, and especially are young students likely to be unable to understand them readily.

The last class of allusions, and one which in books written to-day is especially common, is that which calls up passages or characters in literature itself. We speak of a "quixotic deed;" we allude to a thing as to be taken "in a Pickwickian sense;" we have become so accustomed to hearing a married man spoken of as a "Benedick," that we often forget the brisk and gallant bachelor of "Much Ado about Nothing," and how he was transformed into "Benedick the married man" almost without his own consent. When an author who weighs his words employs allusions of this sort, it is needful to know the originals well if we hope to get the real intent of what is written. In "Il Penseroso," Milton says:—

> Sometime let gorgeous Tragedy
> In sceptered pall come sweeping by,
> Presenting Thebes or Pelops' line,
> Or the tale of Troy divine.

There should pass before the mind of the reader all the fateful story of the ill-starred house of Labdacus: the horrible history of Œdipus, involved in the meshes of destiny; the deadly strife of his sons, and the sublime self-sacrifice of Antigone;

all the involved and passionate tragedies of the descendants of Pelops: Agamemnon, the slaughter of Iphigenia, the vengeance of Clytemnestra, the waiting of Electra, the matricide of Orestes and the descent of the Furies upon him; and after this should come to mind the oft-told tale of Troy in all its fullness. Milton was not one to use words inadvertently or without a clear sense of all that they implied. He desired to suggest all the rich and tragic histories which I have hinted at, to move the reader, and to show how stirring and how pregnant is tragedy when dealing with high themes. In two lines he evokes all that is most potent in Grecian poetry. Or again, when Wordsworth speaks of

> The gentle Lady married to the Moor,
> And heavenly Una with her milk-white lamb,

it is not enough to glance at a foot-note and discover that the allusion is to Desdemona, and to the first canto of Spenser's "Faerie Queene." The reader is expected to be so familiar with the poems referred to that the spirit of one and then of the other comes up to him in all its beauty. An allusion of this sort should be like a breath of perfume which suddenly calls up some dear and thrilling memory.

Enough has been said to show that the language of literature is a complicated and in some respects a difficult one. Literature in its highest and best sense is of an importance and of a value so great as to justify the assumption that no difficulties of language are too great if needed for the full expression of the message which genius bears to mankind. In other words, the writer who can give to his fellows works which are genuinely imaginative is justified in employing any conventions which will really aid in expression. It is the part of his readers to acquaint themselves with the means which he finds it best to employ; and to be grateful for the gift of the master, whatever the trouble it costs to appreciate and to enter into its spirit. If we are wise, if we have a proper sense of values, we shall find it worth our while to familiarize ourselves with scriptural phrases, with mythology, history, folk-lore, or whatever will aid us in seizing the innermost significance of masterpieces.

It is important, moreover, to know literary language before the moment comes for using it. Information grubbed from foot-notes at the instant of need may be better than continued ignorance, but it is impossible to thrill and tingle over a passage in the middle of which allusions must be looked up in the comments of the editor. It is like feeling one's way through a poem in a foreign tongue when one must use a lexicon for every second word. The feelings cannot carry the reader away if they must bear not only the intangible imagination but a solidly material dictionary. As has been said in a former page, notes should not be allowed to interrupt a first reading. It is often a wise plan to study them beforehand, so as to have their aid at once. It is certainly idle to expect a vivid first impression if one stops continually to look up obscure points; one cannot soar to the stars with foot-notes as a flying-machine.

One danger must here be noted. The student may so fill his mind with concern about the language that he cannot give himself up to the author. The language is for the work, and not the work for the language. The teacher who does not instruct the student in the meaning and value of allusion fails of his mission; but the teacher who makes this the limit, and fails to impress upon the learner the fact that all this is a means to an end, commits a crime. I had rather intrust a youth to an instructor ill-informed in the things of which we have been speaking, and filled with a genuine love and reverence for beauty as far as he could apprehend it, than to a preceptor completely equipped with erudition, and filled with Philistine satisfaction over this knowledge for its own sake. No amount of learning can compensate for a lack of enthusiasm. The object of reading literature is not only to understand it, but to experience it; not only to apprehend it with the intellect, but to comprehend it with the emotions. To understand it is necessary and highly important; but this is not the best thing. When the gods send us gifts, let us not be content with examining the caskets.

VIII

THE INTANGIBLE LANGUAGE

WE have spoken of the tangible language of literature; we have now to do with that which is intangible. Open and direct allusion is neither the more important nor the more common form of suggestion. He who has trained himself to recognize references to things historical, mythological, and so on, has not necessarily become fully familiar with literary language. Phrase by phrase, and word by word, literature is a succession of symbols. The aim of the imaginative writer is constantly to excite the reader to an act of creation. He only is a poet who can arouse in the mind a creative imagination. Indeed, one is tempted to indulge here in an impossible paradox, and to say that he only is a poet who can for the time being make his reader a poet also. The object of that which is expressed is to arouse the intellect and the emotions to search for that which is not expressed. The language of allusion is directed to this end, but literature has also its means far more subtile and far more effective.

Suggestion is still the essence of this, but it is suggestion conveyed more delicately and impalpably. Sometimes it is so elusive as almost to seem accidental or even fanciful. The choice of a single word gives to a sentence a character which without it would be entirely wanting; a simple epithet modifies an entire passage. In Lincoln's " Gettysburg Address," for instance, after the so concise and forceful statement of all that has brought the assembly together, the speaker declares "that we here highly resolve that these dead shall not have died in vain." The adverb is the last of which an ordinary mind might have thought in this connection, and yet once spoken, it is the one inevitable and supreme word. It lifts the mind at once into an atmosphere elevated and noble. By this single word Lincoln seems to say: " With the dead at our feet, and the future for which they died before us, lifted by the consciousness of all that their death meant, of all that hangs upon the fidelity with which we carry forward the ideals for which they laid down life itself, we '*highly* resolve that their death shall not have been in vain.'" The phrase is one of the most superb in American literature. It is in itself a trumpet-blast clear and strong. Or take Shakespeare's epithet when he speaks of " death's dateless night." To the appreciative reader this is a word to catch the breath, and to touch one with the horror of that dull darkness where time has ceased; where for the sleeper there is neither end nor beginning, no point distinguished from another; night from which all that makes life has been utterly swept away. " Death's dateless night " !

It is told of Keats that in reading Spenser he

shouted aloud in delight over the phrase "seashouldering whales." The imagination is taken captive by the vigor and vividness of the image of the great monsters shouldering their mighty way through opposing waves as a giant might push his path through a press of armed men, forging onward by sheer force and bulk. The single word says more than pages of ordinary, matter-of-fact description. The reader who cannot appreciate why Keats cried out over this can hardly be said to have begun truly to understand the effect of the epithet in imaginative writing.

Hazlitt cites the lines of Milton : —

> Him followed Rimmon, whose delightful seat
> Was fair Damascus, on the fertile banks
> Of Abbana and Pharphar, lucid streams;

and comments: "The word lucid here gives to the idea all the sparkling effect of the most perfect landscape." In each of the following passages from Shakespeare the single italicized word is in itself sufficient to give distinction : —

> Enjoy the *honey-heavy* dew of slumber.
> *Julius Cæsar*, ii. 1.
>
> When love begins to sicken and decay
> It useth an *enforcèd* ceremony.
> *Ib.*, iv. 2.
>
> After life's *fitful* fever he sleeps well.
> *Macbeth*, iii. 2.

It would lead too far to enter upon the suggestiveness which is the result of skillful use of technical means; but I cannot resist the temptation to call attention to the great effect which may result from a wise repetition of a single word, even if that word be in itself commonplace. I know of nothing else in all literature where so tremendous an effect is produced by simple means as by the use of this device is given in the familiar lines: —

> To-morrow, and to-morrow, and to-morrow,
> Creeps in this petty pace from day to day
> To the last syllable of recorded time.
> *Macbeth*, v. 5.

The suggestion of heart-sick realization of the following of one day of anguish after another seems to sum up in a moment all the woe of years until it is almost more than can be borne.

In many passages appreciation is all but impossible unless the language of suggestion is comprehended. To a dullard there is little or nothing in the line of Chaucer: —

> Up roos the sonne, and up roos Emelye.

It is constantly as important to read what is not written as what is set down. Lowell remarks of Chaucer: "Sometimes he describes amply by the merest hint, as where the Friar, before setting himself softly down, drives away the cat. We know without need of more words that he has chosen the snuggest corner." The richest passages in literature are precisely those which mean so much that to the careless or the obtuse reader they seem to mean nothing.

The great principle of the need of complete comprehension of which we have spoken before meets us here and everywhere. It is necessary to read with a mind so receptive as almost to be creative: creative, that is, in the sense of being able to evoke before the imagination of the reader those things which have been present to the inner vision of the writer. The comprehension of literary language is above all else the power of translating suggestion into imaginative reality.

When we read, for instance : —

> Like waiting nymphs the trees present their fruit;

the line means nothing to us unless we are able with the eye of the mind to see the sentient trees holding out their branches like living arms, tendering their fruits. When Dekker says of patience : —

> 'T is the perpetual prisoner's liberty,
> His walks and orchards;

we do not hold the poet's meaning unless there has come to us a lively sense of how the wretch condemned to life-long captivity may by patience find in the midst of his durance the same buoyant joy which swells in the heart of one who goes with the free step of a master along his own walks and through his richly fruited orchards.

Almost any page of Shakespeare might be given bodily here in illustration. Take, for instance, the talk of Lorenzo and Jessica as in the moonlit garden at Belmont they await the return of Portia.

> *Lor.* The moon shines bright. In such a night as this,
> When the sweet wind did gently kiss the trees,
> And they did make no noise, — in such a night
> Troilus, methinks, mounted the Trojan walls,
> And sighed his soul toward the Grecian tents,
> Where Cressid lay that night.
> *Jes.* . In such a night
> Did Thisbe fearfully o'ertrip the dew,
> And saw the lion's shadow ere himself,
> And ran dismayed away.

Lor.   In such a night
Stood Dido with a willow in her hand
Upon the wild sea-banks, and waved her love
To come again to Carthage.
Jes.   In such a night
Medea gathered the enchanted herbs
That did renew old Æson.

The question is how this is read. Do we go over the enchanting scene mechanically and at speed, as if it were the account of a political disturbance on the borders of Beloochistan? Do we take in the ideas with crude apprehension, satisfied that we are doing our duty to ourselves and to literature because the book which we are thus abusing is Shakespeare? That is one way not to read. Again, we may, with laborious pedantry, discover that all the stories alluded to in this passage are from Chaucer's "Legends of Good Women;" that for a single particular Shakespeare has apparently gone to Gower, but that most of the details he has invented himself. We may look up the accounts of the legendary personages mentioned, compare parallel passages in which they are named, and hunt for the earliest reference to the willow as a sign of woe. There is nothing necessarily vicious in all this. It is a sort of busy idleness which is somewhat demoralizing to the mind, but it is not criminal. It has, it is true, no especial relation to the genuine and proper enjoyment of the poetry. That is a different affair! The reader should luxuriate through the exquisite verse, letting the imagination create fully every image, every emotion. The sense should be steeped in the beauty of that garden, softly distinct in the golden splendors of the moon; there should come again the feeling which has stolen over us on some June night, so lovely that it seemed impossible but that dreams should come true, and in sheer delight of the time we have involuntarily sighed, "In such a night as this!"—as if all that is bewitching and romantic might happen when earth and heaven were attuned to harmony so complete. We should take in the full mood of the lines: —

> When the sweet wind did gently kiss the trees,
> And they did make no noise.

The image of the amorous wind, subduing its riotous glee lest it be overheard, and stealing as it were on tiptoe to kiss the trees, warm and willing in the sweet-scented dusk, makes in the mind the very atmosphere of the sensuous, luscious, moonlit garden at Belmont. We are ready to give our fancy over to the mood of the lovers, and with them to call up the potent images of folk immortal in the old tales: —

> In such a night
> Troilus, methinks, mounted the Trojan walls,
> And sighed his soul toward the Grecian tents,
> Where Cressid lay that night.

If we share the imaginings of the poet, we shall seem to see before us the sheen of the weather-stained Grecian tents, silvered by the moonlight there below the wall where we stand, — we shall seem to stretch unavailing arms toward that far corner of the camp where Cressid must be sleeping, — we shall feel a sigh swell our bosom, and our throat contract.

118 THE STUDY OF LITERATURE

In such a night
Did Thisbe fearfully o'ertrip the dew,
And saw the lion's shadow ere himself,
And ran dismayed away.

The realizing reader moves with timorous eagerness to meet Pyramus, feeling under foot the dew-wet grass and on the cheek the soft night wind, and suddenly, with that awful chill of fright which is like an actual grasp upon the heart, to see the shadow of the lion silhouetted on the turf. He sees with the double vision of the imagination the shrinking, terror-smitten Thisbe, arrested by the shadow at her feet, while also he seems to look through her eyes at the beast which has called up her gaze from the shade to the reality. He trembles with her in a brief-long instant, and then flees in dismay.

Now all this is almost sure to seem to you to be rather closely allied to that pest of teachers of composition which is known as "fine writing." I realize that my comment obscures the text with what is likely to seem a mist of sentimentality. There are two reasons why this should be so, — two, I mean, besides the obvious necessity of failure when we attempt to translate Shakespeare into our own language. In the first place, the feelings involved belong to the elevated, poetic mood, and not at all to dry lecturing. In the second place, and what is of more importance, these emotions can be fairly and effectively conveyed only by suggestion. It is not by specifying love, passion, hate, fear, suspense, and the like, that an author brings them keenly to the mind; but by arousing the reader's imagination to create them. It follows that in insisting upon the necessity of understanding what is connoted as well as what is denoted in what one reads, I am but calling attention to the fact that this is the only way in which the most significant message of a writer may be understood at all. The best of literature must be received by suggestion or missed altogether.

Often ideas which are essential to the appreciation of even the simplest import of a work are conveyed purely by inference. Doubtless most of you are familiar with Rossetti's poem, "Sister Helen." A slighted maiden is by witchcraft doing to death her faithless lover, melting his waxen image before the fire, while he in agony afar wastes away under the eyes of his newly wedded bride as the wax wastes by the flame. Her brother from the gallery outside her tower window calls to her as one after another the relatives of the dying man come to implore her mercy. The first is announced in these words: —

> Oh, it's Keith of Eastholm rides so fast, . . .
> For I know the white mane on the blast.

There follows the plea of the rider, and again the brother speaks: —

> Here's Keith of Westholm riding fast, . . .
> For I know the white plume on the blast.

When the second suppliant has vainly prayed pity, and the third appears, the boy calls to his sister: —

> Oh, it's Keith of Keith now that rides fast, . . .
> For I know the white hair on the blast.

We see first a rider who is not of importance enough to overpower in the mind of the boy the effect of his horse, and we feel instinctively that some younger member of the house has been sent on this errand. Then comes the second brother, and the boy is impressed by the knightly plume, by the trappings of the rider rather than by his personality. An older and more important member of the family has been dispatched as the need has grown greater. It is not, however, until the old man comes, with white locks floating on the wind, that the person of the messenger seizes the attention; it is evident that the head of the house of Keith has come, and that a desperate climax is at hand.

When one considers the care with which writers arrange details like this, of how much depends upon the reader's comprehending them, one knows not whether to be the more angry or the more pitiful in thinking of the careless fashion in which literature is so commonly skimmed over.

It is essential, then, to read carefully and intelligently; and it is no less essential to read imaginatively and sympathetically. Of course the intelligent comprehension of which I am speaking cannot be reached without the use of the imagination. No author can fulfill for you the office of your own mind. In order to accompany an author who soars it is necessary to have wings of one's own. Pegasus is a sure guide through the trackless regions of the sky, but he drags none up after him. The majority of readers are apt unconsciously to assume that a work of imaginative literature is a sort of captive balloon in which any excursionist who is in search of a novel sensation may be wafted heavenward for the payment of a small fee. They sit down to some famous book prepared to be raised far above earth, and they are not only astonished but inclined to be indignant that nothing happens. They feel that they have been defrauded, and that like the prophet Jonah they do well to be angry. The reputation of the masterpiece they regard as a sort of advertisement from which the book cannot fall away without manifest dishonesty on the part of somebody. They are there; they are ready to be thrilled; the reputation of the work guarantees the thrilling; and yet they are unmoved. Straightway they pronounce the reputation of that book a snare and a delusion. They do not in the least appreciate the fact that they have not even learned the language in which the author has written. Literature shows us what we may create for ourselves; it suggests and inspires; it awakens us to the possibilities of life; but the actual act of creation must every mind do for itself. The hearing ear and the responsive imagination are as necessary as the inspired voice to utter high things. You are able appreciatively to read imaginative works when you are able, as William Blake has said: —

> To see the world in a grain of sand,
> And a heaven in a wild flower;
> Hold infinity in the palm of your hand,
> And eternity in an hour.

The language of literature is in reality a tongue as foreign to every-day speech as is the tongue of the folk of another land. It is necessary to learn it as one learns a foreign idiom; and to appreciate the fact that even when it is acquired what we read does not accomplish for us the possibilities of emotion, but only points out the way in which we may rise to them for ourselves.

IX

THE CLASSICS

THE real nature of a classic is perhaps to the general mind even more vague than that of literature. As long as the term is confined to Greek and Roman authors, it is of course simple enough; but the moment the word is given its general and legitimate application the ordinary reader is apt to become somewhat uncertain of its precise meaning. It is not strange, human nature being what it is, that the natural instinct of most men is to take refuge in the idea that a classic is of so little moment that it really does not matter much what it is.

While I was writing these talks, a friend said to me: "I know what I would do if I were to speak about literature. I would tell my audience squarely that all this talk about the superiority of the classics is either superstition or mere affectation. I would give them the straight tip that nobody nowadays really enjoys Homer and Chaucer and Spenser and all those old duffers, and that nobody need expect to." I disregarded the slang, and endeavored to treat this remark with absolute sincerity. It brought up vividly the question which has occurred to most of us how far the often expressed admiration of the classics is genuine. It is impossible not to see that there is a great deal of talk which is purely conventional. We know well enough that the ordinary reader does not take Chaucer or Spenser from the shelf from year's end to year's end. It is idle to deny that the latest novel has a thousand times better chance of being read than any classic, and since there is always a latest novel the classics are under a perpetual disadvantage. How far, then, was my friend right? We live in an age when we dare to question anything; when doubt examines everything. We claim to test things on their merits; and if the reverence with which old authors have been regarded is a mere tradition and a fetish, it is as well that its falsity be known.

Is it true that the majority of readers find the works of the great writers of the past dull and unattractive? I must confess that it is true. It is one of those facts of which we seldom speak in polite society, as we seldom speak of the fact that so large a portion of mankind yield to the temptations of life. It is more of an affront, indeed, to intimate that a man is unfamiliar with Shakespeare than to accuse him of having foully done to death his grandmother. Whatever be the facts, we have tacitly agreed to assume that every intelligent man is of course acquainted with certain books. We all recognize that we live in a society in which familiarity with these works is put forward as an essential condition of intellectual, and indeed almost of social and moral, respectability. One would hesitate to ask to dinner a man who confessed to a complete ignorance of "The Canterbury Tales;" and if one's sister married a person so hardened as to own to being unacquainted with "Hamlet," one would take a good deal of pains to prevent the disgraceful fact from becoming public. We have come to accept a knowledge of the classics as a measure of cultivation; and yet at the same time, by an absurd contradiction, we allow that knowledge to be assumed, and we accept for the real the sham while we are assured of its falsity. In other words, we tacitly agree that cultivation shall be tested by a certain criterion, and then allow men unrebuked to offer in its stead the flimsiest pretext. We piously pretend that we all read the masterpieces of literature while as a rule we do not; and the plain fact is that few of us dare rebuke our neighbors lest we bring to light our own shortcomings.

Such a state of things is sufficiently curious to be worth examination; and there would also seem to be some advisability of amendment. If it is not to be supposed that we can alter public sentiment, we may at least free ourselves from the thralldom of superstition. If this admiration of the classics which men profess with their lips, yet so commonly deny by their acts, is a relic of old-time prejudice, if it be but a mouldy inheritance from days when learning was invested with a sort of supernatural dignity, it is surely time that it was cast aside. We should at least know whether in this matter it is rational to hold by common theory or by common practice.

In the first place it is necessary to supply that definition of a classic which is so generally wanting. In their heart of hearts, concealed like a secret crime, many persons hide an obstinate conviction that a classic is any book which everybody should have read, yet which nobody wishes to read. The idea is not unallied to the notion that goodness is whatever we do not wish to do; and one is as sensible as the other. It has already been said that the object of the study of literature is to enjoy and to experience literature; to live in it and to thrill with its emotions. It follows that the popular idea just mentioned is neither more nor less sensible than the theory that it is better to have lived than to live, to have loved than to love. Whatever else may be said, it is manifest that this popular definition of a classic as a book not to read but to have read is an absurd contradiction of terms.

Equally common is the error that a classic is a book which is merely old. One constantly hears the word applied to any work, copies of which have come down to us from a former generation, with a tendency to assume that merit is in direct proportion to antiquity. To disabuse the mind from this error nothing is needed but to examine intelligently the catalogue of any great library. Therein are to be found lists of numerous authors whose productions have accidentally escaped submergence in the stream of time, and are now preserved as simple and innocuous diet for book-worms insectivorous or human. These writings are not classics, although there is a tribe of busy idlers who devote their best energies to keeping before the public works which have not sufficient vitality to live of themselves, — editors who perform, in a word, the functions of hospital nurses to literary senilities which should be left in decent quiet to die from simple inanition. Mere age no more makes a classic of a poor book than it makes a saint of a sinner.

A classic is more than a book which has been preserved. It must have been approved. It is a work which has received the suffrages of generations. Out of the innumerable books, of the making of which there was no end even so long ago as the days of Solomon, some few have been by the general voice of the world chosen as worthy of preservation. There are certain writings which, amid all the multitudinous distractions of practical life, amid all the changes of custom, belief, and taste, have continuously pleased and moved mankind, — and to these we give the name Classics.

A book has two sorts of interest; that which is temporary, and that which is permanent. The former depends upon its relation to the time in which it is produced. In these days of magazines there is a good deal of talk about articles which are what is called timely. This means that they fall in with some popular interest of the moment. When a war breaks out in the Soudan, an account of recent explorations or travels in that region is timely, because it appeals to readers who just then are eager to increase their information concerning the scene of the disturbance. When there is general discussion of any ethical or emotional topic, the novel or the poem making that topic its theme finds instant response. Often a book of no literary merit whatever speeds forward to notoriety because it is attached, like a barnacle on the side of a ship, to some leading issue of the day. At a time when there is wide discussion of social reforms, for instance, a man might write a rubbishy romance picturing an unhuman and impossible socialism, and find the fiction spring into notoriety from its connection with the theme of popular talk and thought. Books which are really notable, too, may owe their immediate celebrity to connection with some vital topic of the day. Their hold upon later attention will depend upon their lasting merit.

The permanent interest and value of a book are precisely those qualities which have been specified as making it literature. As time goes on all temporary importance fails. Nothing becomes more quickly obsolete than the thing which is merely timely. It may retain interest as a curious historic document. It will always have some value as showing what was read by large numbers at a given period; but nobody will cherish the merely timely book as literature, although in its prime it may have had the widest vogue, and may have conferred upon its author a delicious immortality lasting sometimes half his lifetime. Permanent interest gives a book permanent value, and this depends upon appeal to the permanent characteristics and emotions of humanity.

While the temporary excitement over a book continues, no matter how evanescent the qualities upon which this excitement depends, the reader finds it difficult to realize that the work is not genuine and vital. It is not easy to distinguish the permanent from the momentary interest. With the passage of time extraneous attractions fade, and the work is left to depend upon its essential value. The classics are writings which, when all factitious interests that might have been lent to them by circumstances are stripped away, are found still to be of worth and importance. They are the wheat left in the threshing-floor of time, when has been blown away the chaff of sensational scribblings, noisily notorious productions, and temporary works of what sort soever. It is of course not impossible that a work may have both kinds of merit; and it is by no means safe to conclude that a book is not of enduring worth simply because it has appealed to instant interests and won immediate popularity. "Don Quixote," on the one hand, and "Pilgrim's Progress," on the other, may serve as examples of works which were timely in the best sense, and which yet are permanent literature. The important point is that in the classics we have works which, whether they did or did not receive instant recognition, have by age been stripped of the accidental, and are found worthy in virtue of the essential that remains. They are books which have been proved by time, and have endured the test.

The decision what is and what is not literature may be said to rest with the general voice of the intellectual world. Vague as the phrase may sound, it really represents the shaping power of the thought of the race. It is true that here as in all other matters of belief the general voice is likely to be a confirmation and a repetition of the voice of the few; but whether at the outset indorsed by the few or not, a book cannot be said to be fairly entitled to the name "classic" until it has received this general sanction. Although this sanction, moreover, be as intangible as the wind in a sail, yet like the wind it is decisive and effective.

The leaders of thought, moreover, have not only praised these books and had their judgment indorsed by the general voice, but they have by them formed their own minds. They are unanimous in their testimony to the value of the classics in the development of the perceptions, intellectual and emotional. So universally true is this that to repeat it seems the reiteration of a truism. The fact of which we have already spoken, the fact that those who in theory profess to respect the classics, do yet in practice neglect them utterly, makes it necessary to examine the grounds upon which this truism rests. If the classics are the books which the general voice of the best intelligence of the race has declared to be permanently valuable, if the highest minds have universally claimed to have been nourished and developed by them, why is it that we so often neglect and practically ignore them?

In the first place there are the obstacles of language. There are the so to say technical difficulties of literary diction and form which have been somewhat considered in the preceding talks. There are the greater difficulties of dealing with conceptions which belong to a different mental world. To a savage, the intellectual and emotional experiences of a civilized man would be incomprehensible, no matter in how clear speech they were expressed. To the unimaginative man the life of the world of imagination is pretty nearly as unintelligible as to the bushman of Australian wilds would be the subtly refined distinctions of that now extinct monster, the London æsthete. The men who wrote the classics wrote earnestly and with profound conviction that which they profoundly felt; it is needful to attain to their elevation in point of view before what they have written can be comprehended. This is a feat by no means easy for the ordinary reader. To one accustomed only to facile and commonplace thoughts and emotions it is by no means a light undertaking to rise to the level of the masters. Readers to whom the rhymes of the "poet's corner" in the newspapers, for instance, are thrillingly sweet, are hardly to be expected to be equal to the emotional stress of Shelley's "Prometheus Unbound;" it is not to be supposed that those who find "Over the Hills to the Poor-House" soul-satisfying will respond readily to the poignant pathos of the parting of Hector and Andromache. The admirers of "Curfew must not ring to-night" and the jig-saw school of verse in general are mentally incapable of taking the attitude of genuinely imaginative work. The greatest author can do but so much for his reader. He may suggest, but each mind must for itself be the creator. The classics are those works in which the geniuses of the world have most effectively suggested genuine and vital emotions; but every reader must feel those emotions for himself. Not even the music of the spheres could touch the ear of a deaf man, and for the blind the beauty of Grecian Helen would be no more than ugliness. As Mrs. Browning puts it: —

> What angel but would seem
> To sensual eyes, ghost-dim ?

The sluggish mind is incapable of comprehending, the torpid imagination incapable of realizing; and the struggle to attain to comprehension and to feeling is too great an exertion for the mentally indolent.

It is no less true, that to the mind unused to high emotions the vivid life of imaginative literature is disconcerting. The ordinary reader is as abashed in the presence of these deep and vibrant feelings which he does not understand, and cannot share, as would be an English washerwoman to whom a duchess paid a ceremonious afternoon call. The feeling of inadequacy, of being confronted with an occasion to the requirements of which one is utterly unequal, is baffling and unpleasant to the last degree. In this difficulty of comprehending, and in this inability to feel equal to the demands of the best literature, lies the most obvious explanation of the common neglect of the classics.

It is also true that genuine literature demands for its proper appreciation a mood which is fundamentally grave. Even beneath the humorous runs this vein of serious feeling. It is not possible to read Cervantes or Montaigne or Charles Lamb sympathetically without having behind laughter or smiles a certain inner solemnity. Hidden under the coarse and roaring fun of Rabelais lurk profound observations upon life, which no earnest man can think of lightly. The jests and "excellent fooling" of Shakespeare's clowns and drolls serve to emphasize the deep thought or sentiment which is the real import of the poet's work. Genuine feeling must always be serious, because it takes hold upon the realities of human existence.

It is not that one reading the classics must be sad. Indeed, there is nowhere else fun so keen, humor so exquisite, or sprightliness so enchanting. It is only that human existence is a solemn thing if viewed with a realization of its actualities and its possibilities; and that the great aim of real literature is the presentation of life in its essentials. It is not possible to be vividly conscious of the mystery in the midst of which we live and not be touched with something of awe. From this solemnity the feeble soul shrinks as a silly child shrinks from the dark. The most profound feeling of which many persons are capable is the instinctive desire not to feel deeply. To such readers real literature means nothing, or it means too much. It fails to move them, or it wearies them by forcing them to feel.

Yet another reason for the neglect of the classics is the irresistible attractiveness which belongs always to novelty, which makes a reader choose whatever is new rather than anything which has been robbed of this quality by time. Every mind which is at all responsive is sensitive to this fascination of that which has just been written. What is new borrows importance from the infinite possibilities of the unknown. The secret of life, the great key to all the baffling mysteries of human existence, is still just beyond the bound of human endeavor, and there is always a tingling sense that whatever is fresh may have touched the longed-for solution to the riddle of existence. This zeal for the new makes the old to be left neglected; and while we are eagerly welcoming novelties which in the end too often prove to be of little or no value, the classics, of tried and approved worth, stand in forlorn dust-gathering on the higher shelves of the library.

A. Conan Doyle is reported as saying in a speech before a literary society : —

It might be no bad thing for a man now and again to make a literary retreat, as pious men make a spiritual one; to forswear absolutely for a month in the year all ephemeral literature, and to bring an untarnished mind to the reading of the classics. — *London Academy*, December 5, 1896.

The suggestion is so good that if it does not seem practical, it is so much the worse for the age.

X

THE VALUE OF THE CLASSICS

IT is sufficiently evident that the natural inclinations of the ordinary man are not toward imaginative literature, and that unless there were strong and tangible reasons why it is worth while to cultivate an appreciation and a fondness for them, the classics would be so little read that they might as well be sent to the junk-shop at once, save for the occasional mortal whom the gods from his birth have endowed with the precious gift of understanding high speech. These reasons, moreover, must apply especially to the classics as distinguished from books in general. Briefly stated, some of them are as follows: —

The need of a knowledge of the classics for the understanding of literary language has already been spoken of at some length. This is, of course, a minor and comparatively extraneous consideration, but it is one not to be left wholly out. It is not difficult, however, to get a superficial familiarity with famous writings by means of literary dictionaries and extract books; and with this a good many persons are apparently abundantly content. The process bears the same relation to the actual study of the originals that looking at foreign photographic views does to traveling abroad. It is undoubtedly better than nothing, although it is by no means the real thing. It gives one an intellectual understanding of classic and literary allusions, but not an emotional one. Fully to appreciate and enjoy the allusions with which literature is filled, it is essential to have gained knowledge directly from the originals.

One reason why references to the classics are so frequent in literary language, is that in these writings are found thought and emotional expression in their youth, so to say. Even more important than learning the force of these allusions is the coming in contact with this fresh inspiration and utterance. That into which a man steps full grown can never be to him the same as that in which he has grown up. We cannot have with the thing which we have known only in its complete form the same intimate connection as with that which we have watched from its very beginnings. To that with which we have grown we are united by a thousand delicate and intangible fibres, fine as cobweb and strong as steel. The student who attempts to form himself solely upon the literature of to-day misses entirely the childhood, the youth, the growth of literary art. He comes full grown, and generally sophisticated, to that which is itself full grown and sophisticated. It is not possible for him to become himself a child, but he may go back toward the childhood of emotional expression and as it were advance step by step with the race. He may feel each fresh emotional discovery as if it were as new to him as it was in truth new for the author who centuries ago expressed it so well that the record has become immortal.

I do not know whether what I mean is fully clear, and it is of course difficult to give examples where the matter is so subtle. It is certain, however, that any reader of early literature must be conscious how in the simplicity and naïveté of the best old authors we find things which are now hackneyed and all but commonplace said with a freshness and conviction which makes them for the first time real to us. Many emotions have been so long recognized and expressed in literature that there seems hardly to be a conceivable phase in which they have not been shown, and hardly a conceivable phrase in which they have not been embodied. It appears impossible to express them now with the freshness and sincerity which belonged to them when they were first imprisoned in words. So true is this that were it not that the personal impress of genius and the experience of the imaginative writer always give vitality, literature would cease from the face of the earth, and become a lost art.

It is the persuasion and vividness of first discovery which impart to the folk-song its charm and force. The early ballads often put to shame the poetry of later days. The unsophisticated singers of these lays had never been told that it was proper for them to have any especial emotions; they had never heard talk about this feeling or that, and art did not consciously exist for them as other than the spontaneous and sincere expression of what really moved them. That which they felt too strongly to repress, they said without any self-consciousness. Their artistic forms were so simple as to impose no hindrance to the instinctive desire for revealing to others what swelled in their very hearts. The result is that impressiveness and that convincingness which can come from nothing but perfect sincerity. Innumerable poets have put into verse the sentiments of the familiar folk-song, "Waly, waly;" yet it is not easy to find in all the list the same thing said with a certain childlike directness which goes to the heart that one finds in passages like this: —

> O waly, waly, but love be bonny
> A little time while it is new;
> But when 't is auld, it waxeth cauld,
> And fades awa' like morning dew!

What later singer is there who has surpassed in pathos that makes the heart ache the exquisite beauty of "Fair Helen"?

> I would I were where Helen lies;
> Night and day on me she cries;
> Oh, that I were where Helen lies
> On fair Kirconnell Lea! . . .
>
> I would I were where Helen lies;
> Night and day on me she cries;
> And I am weary of the skies,
> Since my love died for me.

The directness and simplicity which are the charm of folk-song and ballad are far more likely to be found in early literature than in that which is produced under conditions which foster self-consciousness. They belong, it is true, to the work of all really great writers. No man can produce genuinely great art without being completely possessed by the emotions which he expresses; so that for the time being he is not wholly removed from the mood of the primitive singers. Singleness of purpose and simplicity of expression, however, are the birthright of those writers who have been pioneers in literature. It is chiefly in their work that we may hope to experience the delight of finding emotions in the freshness of their first youth, of gaining something of that realization of perception which is fully only his who first of mortal men discovers and proclaims some new possibility of human existence.

Another quality of much importance in primitive writings and the early classics is complete freedom from sentimentality. As certain parasites do not attack young trees, so sentimentality is a fungus which never appears upon a literature until it is well grown. It is not until a people is sufficiently cultivated to appreciate the expression of emotions in art that it is capable of imitating them or of simulating that which it has learned to regard as a desirable or noble feeling. As cultivation advances, there is sure to be at length a time when those who have more vanity than sentiment begin to affect that which it has come to be considered a mark of high cultivation to feel. We all know this vice of affectation too well, and I mention it only to remark that from this literature in its early stages is far more apt to be free than it is in its later and more consciously developed phases.

The blight which follows sentimentality is morbidity; and one of the most important characteristics of the genuine classics is their wholesome sanity. By sanity I mean freedom from the morbid and the diseased; and the quality is one especially to be prized in these days of morbid tendencies and diseased eccentricities. There is much in many of the classics which is sufficiently coarse when measured by later and more refined standards; but even this is free from the gangrene which has developed in over-ripe civilizations. Rabelais chose the dung-hill as his pulpit; in Shakespeare and Chaucer and Homer and in the Bible there are many things which no clean-minded man would now think of saying; but there is in none of these any of that insane pruriency which is the chief claim to distinction of several notorious contemporary authors. Neither is there in classic writers the puling, sentimental, sickly way of looking at life as something all awry. The reader who sits down to the Greek poets, to Dante, to Chaucer, to Molière, to Shakespeare, to Cervantes, to Montaigne, to Milton, knows at least that he is entering an atmosphere wholesome, bracing, and manly, free alike from sentimentality and from all morbid and insane taint.

Besides a knowledge of literary language, we must from the classics gain our standards of literary judgment. This follows from what has been said of temporary and permanent interest in books. Only in the classics do we find literature reduced to its essentials. The accidental associations which cluster about any contemporary work, the fleeting value which this or that may have from accidental conditions, the obscurity into which prejudice of a particular time may throw real merit, all help to make it impossible to learn from contemporary work what is really and essentially bad or good. It is from works which may be looked at dispassionately, writings from which the accidental has been stripped by time, that we must inform ourselves what shall be the standard of merit. It is only from the classics that we may learn to discriminate the essential from the incidental, the permanent from the temporary; and thus gain a criterion by which to try the innumerable books poured upon us by the inexhaustible press of to-day.

Nor do we gain only standards of literature from the classics, but standards of life as well. In a certain sense standards of literature and of life may be said to be one, since our estimate of the truth and the value of a work of art and our judgment of the meaning and value of existence can hardly be separated. The highest object for which we study any literature being to develop character and to gain a knowledge of the conditions of being, it follows that it is for these reasons in especial that we turn to the classics. These works are the verdicts upon life which have been most generally approved by the wisest men who have lived; and they have been tested not by the experiences of one generation only, but by those of succeeding centuries. For wise, wholesome, and comprehensive living there is no better aid than a familiar, intimate, sympathetic knowledge of the classics.

XI

THE GREATER CLASSICS

THERE are, then, clear and grave reasons why the classics are worthy of the most intelligent and careful attention. The evidence supports cultivated theory rather than popular practice. We are surely right in the most exacting estimate of the place that they should hold in our lives; and in so far as we neglect them, in so far we are justly condemned by the general if vague opinion of society at large. They are the works to which apply with especial force whatever reasons there are which give value to literature; they are the means most efficient and most readily at hand for the enriching and the ennobling of life.

It is impossible here to specify to any great extent what individual books among the classics are of most importance. This has been done over and over, and it is within the scope of these talks to do little more than to consider the general relation to life of the study of literature. Some, however, are of so much prominence that it is impossible to pass them in silence. There are certain works which inevitably come to the mind as soon as one speaks of the classics at all; and of these perhaps the most prominent are the Bible, Homer, Dante, Chaucer, and Shakespeare. The Greek tragedians, Boccaccio, Molière, Cervantes, Montaigne, Spenser, Milton, Ariosto, Petrarch, Tasso, and the glorious company of other writers, such as the Elizabethan dramatists and the few really great Latin authors, it seems almost inexcusable not to discuss individually, yet they must be passed over here. The simple lists of these men and their works give to the mind of the genuine book-lover a glow as if he had drunk of generous wine. No man eager to get the most from life will pass them by; but in these talks there is not space to consider them particularly.

Although it is only with its literary values that we have at present any concern, it is somewhat difficult to speak of the Bible from a merely literary point of view. Those who regard the Bible as an inspired oracle are apt to forget that it has too a literary worth, distinct from its religious function, and they are inclined to feel somewhat shocked at any discussion which even for the moment leaves its ethical character out of account. On the other hand, those who look upon the Scriptures as the instrument of a theology of which they do not approve are apt in their hostility to be blind to the literary importance and excellence of the work. There is, too, a third class, perhaps to-day, and especially among the rising generation, the most numerous of all, who simply neglect the Bible as dull and unattractive, and made doubly so by the iteration of appeals that it be read as a religious guide. Undoubtedly this feeling has been fostered by the injudicious zeal of many of the friends of the book, who have forced the Scriptures forward until they have awakened that impulse of resistance which is the instinctive self-preservation of individuality. In all these classes for different reasons praise of the Bible is likely to awaken a feeling of opposition; yet the fact remains that from a purely literary point of view the Bible is the most important prose work in the language.

The rational attitude of the student toward the Scriptures is that which separates entirely the religious from the literary consideration. I wish to speak on the same footing to those who do and those who do not regard the Bible as a sacred book, with those who do and those who do not receive its religious teachings. Let for the moment these points be waived entirely, and there remains the splendid literary worth of this great classic; there remains the fact that it has shaped faith and fortune for the whole of Europe and America for centuries; and especially that the English version has been the most powerful of all intellectual and imaginative forces in moulding the thought and the literature of all English-speaking peoples. One may regard the theological effects of the Scriptures as altogether admirable, or one may feel that some of them have been narrowing and unfortunate; one may reject or accept the book as a religious authority; but at least one must recognize that it is not possible to enter upon the intellectual and emotional heritage of the race without being acquainted with the King James Bible.

"Intense study of the Bible," Coleridge has said most justly, "will keep any writer from being vulgar in point of style." He might almost have added that appreciative study of this book will protect any reader from vulgarity in literature and life alike. The early sacred writings of any people have in them the dignity of sincere conviction and imaginative emotion. The races to which these books have been divine have revered them as the word of the Deity, but it is the supreme emotion which thrills through them that has touched their readers and made possible and real the claim of inspiration. Every responsive reader must vibrate with the human feeling of which they are full. We are little likely to have anything but curiosity concerning the dogmas of the ancient Hindoo or Persian religion, yet it is impossible to read the ecstatic hymns of the Vedas or the exalted pages of the Zend-Avesta without being profoundly moved by the humanity which cries out in them. Of the Bible this is especially true for us, because the book is so closely connected with the life and development of our branch of the human family.

If it were asked which of the classics a man absolutely must know to attain to a knowledge of literature even respectable, the answer undoubtedly would be: "The Bible and Shakespeare." He must be familiar — familiar in the sense in which we use that word in the phrase, "mine own familiar friend, in whom I trusted" — with the greatest plays of Shakespeare, and with the finer portions of the Scriptures. I do not of course mean all of the Bible. Nobody, no matter how devout, can be expected to find imaginative stimulus in strings of genealogies such as that which begins the Book of Chronicles, or in the minute details of the Jewish ceremonial law. I mean the simple directness of Genesis and Exodus ; the straightforward sincerity of Judges and Joshua ; the sweetness and beauty of Ruth and Esther ; the passionately idealized sensuousness of Canticles ; the shrewdly pathetic wisdom of Ecclesiastes ; the splendidly imaginative ecstasies of Isaiah ; the uplift of the Psalms ; the tender virility of the Gospels ; the spiritual dithyrambics of the Apocalypse. No reader less dull than a clod can remain unreverent and unthrilled in the presence of that magnificent poem which one hesitates to say is surpassed by either Homer or Dante, the Book of Job. The student of literature may be of any religion or of no religion, but he must realize, and realize by intimate acquaintance, that, taken as a whole, the Bible is the most virile, the most idiomatic, the most imaginative prose work in the language.

The appearance of literary editions of portions of the Bible for general reading is an encouraging sign that there is to-day a reaction from the neglect into which the book has fallen. Unfortunately, these editions follow for the most part the text of the Revised Version, which may be excellent from a theological point of view, but which from a literary one stands in much the same relation to the King James version as the paraphrases of Dryden stand to the original text of Chaucer.

The literary student is concerned with the book which has been in the hands and hearts of writers and thinkers of preceding generations; with the words which have tinctured the prose masterpieces and given color to the poetry of our tongue. To attempt to alter the text now is for the genuine literary student not unlike modernizing Shakespeare.

The Bible is a library in itself, so great is its variety; and it is practically indispensable as a companion in literary study. To neglect it is one of the most grave errors possible to the student. It has, it is true, its serious and obvious defects, and from a literary point of view the New Testament is infinitely less interesting than the Old; but taken all in all, it is a great and an enchanting book, permanent in its worth and permanent in its interest.

To go on to talk of Homer is at once to bring up the much-vexed question of reading translations. It seems to me rather idle in these days to take time to discuss this. Whatever decision be arrived at, the fact remains that the general reader will not read the classics in the original. However great the loss, he must take them in the English version, or let them alone. Even the most accomplished graduates of the best colleges are not always capable of appreciating in Greek the literary flavor of the works which they can translate pretty accurately. There is no longer time in these busy and over-crowded days for the student so to saturate himself with a dead language that it shall be as familiar to him as his own tongue. The multiplicity of present impressions renders it all but impossible to get completely into the atmosphere of a civilization bygone. A few of the men trained in foreign schools in the most scholarly fashion have probably arrived at the power of feeling sensitively the literary quality of the classics in the original; but for the ordinary student, this is entirely out of the question. It is sad, but it is an inevitable human limitation. Emerson, as is well known, boldly commended the practice of reading translations. His sterling sense probably desired the consistency of having theory agree with practice where there is not the slightest hope of making practice agree with theory. Whether we like it or do not like it, the truth is that most persons will take the Greek and Latin authors in translation or not at all.

And certainly they must be read in some tongue. No genuine student of literature will neglect Homer or the Greek tragedians. The old Greeks were by no means always estimable creatures. They not infrequently did those things which they ought not to have done, and left undone those things which they ought to have done; but the prayer-book did not then exist, so that in spite of all there was plenty of health in them. They were not models in morals, while they were entirely unacquainted with many modern refinements; but they were eminently human. They were sane and wholesome beings, manly and womanly; so that a reader is in far better company with the heroes of Homer in their vices than he is with the morbid creations of much modern fiction in their moments of the most conscious and painfully elaborated virtue. Herein, it seems to me, lies the greatest value of Greek literature. Before he can be anything else thoroughly and soundly, a man must be healthily human. Hot-house virtue is on the whole about as dangerous a disease as open-air vice; and it is far more difficult to cure. Unless a man or a woman be genuine, he or she is nothing, and the mere appearance of good or evil is not of profound consequence. To be sane and human, to think genuine thoughts, and to do genuine deeds, is the beginning of all real virtue; and nothing is more conducive to the development of genuineness than the company of those who are sound and real. If we are with whole-souled folk, we cannot pose, even to ourselves; and it seems to me that the reader who, with full and buoyant imagination, puts himself into the company of the Greeks of Homer or Æschylus or Euripides or Sophocles cannot be content, for the time being at least, to be anything but a simply genuine human creature himself.

Of course I do not mean that the reader reasons this out. Consciously to think that we will be genuine is dangerously near a pose in itself. It is that he finds himself in a company so thoroughly manly, so real and virile, that he instinctively will take long breaths, and without thinking of it lay aside the conventional pose which self is so apt to impose upon self. We do not, while reading, lose in the least the power of judging between right and wrong. We realize that Ulysses, delightful old rascal though he is, is an unconscionable trickster. We are no more likely to play fast and loose with domestic ties because the Grecian heroes, and even the Greek gods, left their morals at home for their wives to keep bright while they went abroad to take their pleasure. Manners and standards in those days were not altogether the same that they are now; but right is right in Homer, and wrong is wrong, as it is in the work of every really great poet since the world began. The whole of Greek poetry, like Greek sculpture, has an enchanting and wholesome open-air quality; and even when it is nude it is not naked. We miss much of the beauty by losing the wonderful form, and no translation ever approached the original, but we get always the mood of sanity and reality.

The mood of Dante seems sometimes more difficult for the modern reader than that of the Greeks. The high spiritual severity, the passionate austerity of the Florentine, are certainly far removed from the busy, practical temper of to-day. Far away as they are in time, the Greeks were after all men of tangible deeds, of practical affairs; they knew the taste of ginger hot i' the mouth, and took hold upon life with a zest thoroughly to be appreciated in this materialistic age. Dante, on the other hand, has the burning solemnity of the prophets of the Old Testament, so that the point of view of the "Divine Comedy" is not far removed from that of Isaiah. Of all the greatest classics the

"Divine Comedy" is probably the least read today, at any rate in this country. The translations of it are for the most part hopelessly unsatisfactory, the impossibility of setting poetry over from the honeyed Italian into a language of a genius so different as the English being painfully obvious even to those little critical. There is a great deal that is obscure, and yet more which cannot be understood without a good deal of special historical information; so that it is impossible to read Dante for the first time without that frequent reference to the notes which is so unfortunate and undesirable in a first reading. It is practically necessary to go over the notes with care once or twice before attempting the poem. Get the information first, and then plunge into the poetry. It is a plunge into a sea whereof the brine is bitter, the waters piercingly cold, and where not infrequently the waves roll high; but it is a plunge invigorating and life-giving. The man who has once read Dante with sympathy and delight can never again be wholly common and unclean, no matter into what woful faults and follies he may thereafter fall.

To come nearer home, readers are somewhat foolishly apt to feel that it is about as difficult to read Chaucer as it is to read Homer or Dante. As a matter of fact any intelligent and educated person should be able to master the theories of the pronunciation of Chaucerian English in a couple of mornings, and to read him with ease and pleasure in a week or two at most. It is a pity that there is not a good complete edition of Chaucer pointed and accented, so that the reader might not be troubled with any consciousness of effort; but after all, the difficulty lies more in the idea than in the fact. When one has mastered the language of the thirteenth century, in company how enchanting does he find himself! The sweetness, the wholesomeness, the kindliness, the sincerity, the humor, and the humanity of Chaucer can hardly be overpraised.

Of Shakespeare, — " our myriad-minded Shakespeare," — it seems almost needless to speak. Concerning his poetry one may be silent because the theme is so wide, and because writers so many and so able have already discoursed upon the subject so eloquently. To attempt to-day to explain why men should read Shakespeare is like entering into an argument to prove that men should delight in the sunshine or to explain that the sea is beautiful and wonderful. If readers to-day neglect this supreme classic it is not from ignorance of its importance. It may be from a want of realization of the pleasure and inspiration which the poet affords. Those who have not tested it may doubt as one heart-whole doubts the joys of love, and in either case only experience can make wise.

Dryden's words may suffice here and stand for all the quotations which might be made : —

To begin with Shakespeare. He was the man who of all modern and perhaps ancient poets had the largest and most comprehensive soul. All the images of nature were still present to him, and he drew them not laboriously, but luckily: when he describes anything you more than see it, you feel it.

The man who does not read and delight in this poet is scarcely to be considered intellectually alive at all, as far as there is any connection between the mind and literature; and the highest intellectual crime of which an English-speaking man is capable is to leave his Shakespeare to gather dust upon his shelves unread.

In all this I do not wish to be understood as holding that we are always to read the classics, or that we are to read nothing else. To live up to the requirements of the society of Apollo continuously would be too fatiguing even for the Muses. We cannot be always in a state of exaltation; but we cannot in any high sense live at all without becoming familiar with what exalted living is. The study of the classics calls for conscious and often for strong endeavor. We do not put ourselves thoroughly into the mood of other times and of remote conditions without effort. Indeed, it requires effort to lift our less buoyant imaginations to the level of any great work. The sympathetic reading of any supremely imaginative author is like climbing a mountain, — it is not to be accomplished without strain, but it rewards one with the breath of an upper air and a breadth of view impossible in the valley. For him who prefers the outlook of the earth-worm to that of the eagle the classics have no message and no meaning. For him who is not content with any view save the widest, these are the mountain peaks which lift to the highest and noblest sight.

XII

CONTEMPORARY LITERATURE

WE speak of the classics, of ancient literature, and of contemporary literature, but in reality all literature is one. We divide it into sections for convenience of study, but it is a notable error to forget that it is consecutive from the dawn of civilization to the present. It is true that in applying the term to works of our own time it is both customary and necessary to employ the word with a meaning wider than that which it has elsewhere. It is often difficult to distinguish in contemporary productions that which is of genuine and lasting merit from that which is simply meretricious and momentary, and still harder to force others to recognize such distinction when made. It is therefore inevitable that the name literature should have a broader signification than when applied to work which has been tested and approved by time.

There are few things more perplexing than the attempt to choose from the all but innumerable books of our own day those which are to be considered as genuine. If we are able to keep vividly in mind what qualities make a thing literature, it is possible to have some not inadequate idea of what contemporary writings most completely fulfill the given conditions. We are able to speak with assurance of the work of a Tennyson or a Browning; and to feel that we have witnessed the birth of classics of the future. Beside these, however, stand the enormous multitude of books which are widely read, much talked about, and voluminously advertised; books which we cannot openly dispraise without the risk of being sneered at as captious or condemned as conceited. There are the poems which publishers inform the public in column-long advertisements, bristling with the testimonials of men and women who make writing their business, are the finest productions since Shakespeare; there are the novels which prove themselves to be works of genius by selling by the hundreds of thousands of copies and very likely being given to the purchasers of six bars of some patent soap; there are the thin and persecuted looking volumes of "prose poems" or rhyming prose which are looked upon by small bands of devoted followers as the morsel of leaven which is to leaven the whole lump; there are, in short, all those perplexing writings which have merit of some kind and in some degree, yet to decide the genuine and lasting merit of which might tax the wisdom and the patience of a Solomon of Solomons.

I have already spoken of the effect which temporary qualities are sure to have in determining the success of an author. The history of books is full of instances of works which have in their brief day filled the reading world with noisy admiration, but which have in the end been found destitute of enduring merit. While transient fame is at its height, while enthusiastically injudicious admirers are praising and judiciously enthusiastic publishers are reëchoing their plaudits, it is a well-trained mind that is able to form a sound and rational judgment, and to distinguish between the ephemeral and the abiding. The only hope lies in a careful and discriminating application of standards deduced from the classics. He who desires to judge the books of to-day must depend upon comparison with the books of yesterday. He must be able to feel toward the literature of the past as if it were of the present, and toward that of the present as if it were of the past.

It is not to the popular verdict upon a work that one can look for aid in deciding upon real merit. In time the general public accepts the verdict of the few, but at first it is the noisy opinion of the many, voluble and undiscriminating, which is heard. The general public is always affected more by the accidental than by the permanent qualities of a work, and it is more often imposed upon by shams than touched by real feeling. It is easy to recognize conventional signs for sentiment, and it is not difficult for the ordinary reader to persuade himself that he experiences emotions which are explicitly set forth for him. Popular taste and popular power of appreciation are not inaccurately represented by those eminently successful journals which in one column give the fashions and receipts for cake and in the next detailed directions for experiencing all the sensations of culture. Sentimentality is always more instantly and more widely effective than sentiment. Sentimentality finds a ready response from the fact that it only calls upon us to seem, while sentiment demands that for the time being at least we shall be.

It is necessary here to say that I do not wish to be misunderstood. I do not mean in the least to speak with scorn or contempt of the lack of power justly to discriminate and to appreciate which comes from either natural disability or lack of opportunities of cultivation. Narrowness of comprehension and appreciation is a misfortune, but it is not necessarily a fault. I mean only to point out that it is a thing to be outgrown if possible. Of the pathos of lives which are denied their desire in this I am too keenly aware to speak of such otherwise than tenderly. For the young women who put their sentiments up in curl-papers and the young men who wax the mustaches of their minds I have no patience whatever; but for those who are seeking that which seems to them the best, even though they blunder and mistakenly fall prostrate before Dagon, the great god of the Philistines, it is impossible not to feel sympathy and even admiration. In what I have been saying of the fallibility of popular opinion I have not meant to cast scorn on any sincerity, no matter where it is to be found; but merely to point out that the general voice of the public, even when sincere, is greatly to be distrusted.

Whatever contemporary literature may be, however mistaken may be the popular verdict, and however difficult it may be for the most careful criticism to determine what is of lasting and what of merely ephemeral merit, the fact remains that it is the voice of our own time, and as such cannot be disregarded. To devote attention exclusively to the classics is to get out of sympathy with the thought of our own generation. It is idle to expend energy in learning how to live if one does not go on to live. The true use of literature is not to make dreamers; it is not to make the hold upon actual existence less firm. In the classics one learns what life is, but one lives in his own time. It follows that no man can make his intellectual life full and round who does not keep intelligently in touch with what is thought and what is written by the men who are alive and working under the same conditions.

Contemporary literature is the expression of the convictions of the time in which it is written. The race having advanced so far, this is the conclusion to which thinkers have come in regard to the meaning of life. Contemporary literature is like news from the front in war-time. It is sometimes cheering, sometimes depressing, often enough inaccurate, but continually exciting. It is the word which comes to us of the progress of the eternal combat against the unknown forces of darkness which compass humanity around. There are many men who make a good deal of parade of never reading books of their own time. They are sometimes men of no inconsiderable powers of intellect and of much cultivation; but it is hardly possible to regard them as of greater contemporary interest than are the mummies of the Pharaohs. They may be excellent in their day and generation, but they have deliberately chosen that their generation shall be one that is gone and their day a day that is ended. They may be interesting relics, but relics they are. It is often wise to wait a time for the subsiding of the frenzy of applause which greets a book that is clever or merely startling. It is not the lover of literature who reads all the new books because they are new, any more than it is he who neglects the old because they are old; but if we are alive and in sympathy with our kind, we cannot but be eager to know what the intellectual world is thinking, what are the fresh theories of life, born of added experience, what are the emotions of our own generation. We cannot, in a word, be in tune with our time without being interested in contemporary literature.

It is here that the intellectual character of a man is most severely tested. Here he is tried as by fire, and if there be in him anything of sham or any flaw in his cultivation it is inevitably manifest. It is easy to know what to read in the classics; they are all explicitly labeled by the critics of succeeding generations. When it comes to contemporary work a reader is forced largely to depend upon himself. Here he must judge by his individual standards; and here he both must and will follow his own inclinations. It is not always possible for a man accurately to appraise his mental advancement by the classics he reads, because his choice may there be influenced by conventional rather than by personal valuation; but if he will compare with the established classics the books which he genuinely likes and admires among the writings of his own time, he may come at an estimate of his mental state as fair as a man is ever likely to form of himself.

It is, then, easy to see that there is a good deal of danger in dealing with current work. It is necessary to be in sympathy with the thought of the day, but it is only too common to pay too dear for this. It is extremely hard, for instance, to distinguish between genuine literary taste and curiosity when writings are concerned which have the fresh and lively interest which attaches to those things about which our fellows are actually talking and thinking. It is of course allowable to gratify a healthy curiosity, but it is well to recognize that such reading is hardly likely to promote mental growth. There is no law, civil or moral, against indulging the desire to know what is in any one of those books which are written to be talked about at ladies' luncheons; and it is not impossible that the readers who give their time to this unwholesome stuff would be doing something worse if they were not reading it. The only point upon which I wish to insist is that such amusement is neither literary nor intellectual.

There is, moreover, the danger of allowing the mind to become fixed upon the accidental instead of the permanent. I have spoken of the fact that the temporary interest of a book may be so great as to blind the reader to all else. When "Uncle

Tom's Cabin" was new, it was practically impossible for the readers of that day to see in it anything but a fiery tract against slavery. To-day who reads "Ground Arms" without being chiefly impressed with its arguments against war? It is as controversial documents that these books were written. If they have truth to life, if they adequately express human emotion, they will be of permanent value after this temporary interest has passed. The danger is that the passing interest, which is natural and proper in itself, shall blind us to false sentiment, to unjust views of life, to sham emotion. We are constantly led to forget the important principle that books of our own time must be judged by the standards which are afforded by the books which are of all time.

There has never been a time when self-possession and sound judgment in dealing with contemporary literature were more important than they are to-day. The immeasurably prolific press of the nineteenth century is like a fish-breeding establishment where minnows are born by the million a minute. There are so many books that the mind becomes bewildered. The student who might have the strength of mind to form an intelligent opinion of five books is utterly incapable of doing the same by five thousand. We are all constantly led on to read too many things. It has been again and again remarked that our grandfathers were better educated than their grandsons because they knew thoroughly the few works which came in their way. We have become the victims of over-reading until the modern mind seems in danger of being destroyed by literary gluttony.

It is well in dealing with contemporary work to be especially self-exacting in insisting that a book is not to be read once which is not to be read a second time. This may seem to be a rule made merely for the sake of having a proper theory, yet it is to be taken literally and observed exactly. It is true that the temptation is so great to read books which are talked about, that we are all likely to run through a good many things which we know to be really unworthy of a single perusal, and of course to go over them again would be a waste of more time. Where to draw the line between the permanent and the ephemeral is a point which each must settle for himself. If, on the whole, it seem to a man well to pay the price in time and in the risk of forming bad mental habits, it is his right to do this, but pay the price he must and will.

It is hardly possible to discuss contemporary literature without speaking of that which is not literature, — the periodicals. One of the conditions of the present time which most strongly affects the relations of ordinary readers to reading in general is the part which periodicals of one sort or another play in modern life. The newspaper enters so intimately into existence to-day that no man can escape it if he would, and with innumerable readers it is practically the sole mental food. It is hardly necessary to say that there is no more relation between the newspaper and literature than there would be between two persons because they both wear hats. Both books and journals are expressed in printed words, and that is about all that there is in common. It is necessary to use the daily paper, but its office is chiefly a mechanical one. It is connected with the purely material side of life. This is not a fault, any more than it is the fault of a spade that it is employed to dig the earth instead of being used to serve food with. It is not the function of the newspapers to minister to the intellect or the imagination in any high sense. They fulfill their mission when they are clean and reliable in material affairs. What is beyond this is a pretense at literature under impossible conditions, assumed to beguile the unwary, and harmless or vicious, according to circumstances. It is seen at its worst in the Sunday editions, with their sheets as many

— as autumnal leaves that strow the brooks
In Vallombrosa.

It is safe to say that for the faithful reader of the Sunday newspaper there is no intellectual salvation. Like the Prodigal Son, he is fain to fill his belly with the husks which the swine do eat, and he has not the grace even to long for the more dignified diet of fatted calf.

The newspaper habit is pretty generally recognized as demoralizing, and in so far it may be in a literary point of view less dangerous than the magazine habit. The latter is often accompanied by a self-righteous conviction that it is a virtue. There is a class who take on airs of being of the intellectual elect on the strength of reading all the leading magazines; who are as proud of having four serials in hand at once as is a society belle of being able to drive as many horses; who look with a sort of pitying contempt upon persons so old-fashioned as to neglect the magazines in favor of books, and who in general are as proudly patronizing in their attitude toward literature as they are innocent of any connection with it. This is worse than too great a fondness for journalism, and of course this is an extreme type; but it is to be feared that at their best the magazines represent mental dissipation.

It is true that genuine literature is often published in periodicals; and there are many editors who deeply regret that the public will not allow them to print a great deal more. As things are, real literature in the magazines is the exception rather than the rule. The general standard of magazine excellence is the taste of the intellectually *nouveaux riches* — for persons who have entered upon an intellectual heritage which they are not fitted rightly to understand or employ are as common as those who come to material wealth under the same conditions. It is to this class, which is one of the most numerous, and still more one of the most conspicuous in our present civilization, that most of the magazines address themselves. The genuinely cultivated reader finds in the monthlies many papers which he looks through as he looks through the newspaper, for the sake of information, and less often he comes upon imaginative work. The serials which are worth reading at all are worthy of being read as a whole, and not in the distorted and distorting fashion of so many words a month, according to the size of the page of a particular periodical. Reading a serial is like plucking a rose petal by petal; the whole of the flower may be gathered, but its condition is little likely to be satisfactory. While the magazines, moreover, are not to be looked to for a great deal of literature of lasting value, they not only encourage the habit of reading indifferent imitations, but they foster a dangerous and demoralizing inability to fix the attention for any length of time. The magazine-mind is a thing of shreds and patches at best; incapable of grasping as a whole any extended work. Literature holds the mirror up to nature, but the magazine is apt to show the world through a toy multiplying-glass, which gives to the eye a hundred minute and distorted images.

It may seem that I do scant justice to the magazines. It is certainly to be remembered that in the less thickly settled parts of this great inchoate country, where libraries are not, the magazine is often a comfort and even an inspiration. It is to be acknowledged that, with the enormous mass of half-educated but often earnest and sincere souls, the periodical has done and may still do a great deal of good. The child must play with toys before it is fitted to grasp the tools of handicraft, and enjoyment of the chromo may be a healthy and legitimate stage on the way to an appreciation of the masters of painting. It is not a reproach to call a man a toy-vender or a maker of chromos;

nor do I see that what I have been saying is to be interpreted as reflecting on the makers of periodicals. It must be remembered that the publication of a magazine is a business enterprise in the same sense that the selling of carpets or calicoes is a business enterprise. The manufacturer of magazines must please the general public with what he prints, as the manufacturer must satisfy the ordinary buyer by the designs of his fabrics. In either case it is the taste of the intellectual *bourgeoisie* which is the standard of success. The maker of periodicals can no more afford to appeal to the taste of the cultivated few than can the thrifty maker of stuffs. What is sold in open market must be adapted to the demands of the open market. It is simply legitimate business prudence which keeps most magazines from attempting to print literature. They publish, as a rule, all the literature that the public will have, — modified, unhappily, by the difficulty of getting it to publish in a world where literature cannot be made to order. A book, it is to be remembered, is a venture; a magazine is an enterprise. The periodical must pay or it must be discontinued.

The moral of the whole matter is that the only thing to do is to accept magazines for what they are; neither to neglect them completely, nor to give to them that abundant or exclusive attention which they cannot even aim under existing conditions at deserving. They may easily be dangerous intellectual snares; but the wise student will often find them enjoyable, and sometimes useful.

XIII

NEW BOOKS AND OLD

THE quality of "timeliness" is one of the things which makes it especially difficult to distinguish among new books. There is in this day an ever increasing tendency to treat all topics of popular discussion in ways which profess to be imaginative, and especially in the narrative form. The novel with a theory and the poem with a purpose are so enveloped with the glamour of immediate interest that they appear to be of an importance far beyond that which belongs to their real merit. Curiosity to know what these books have to say upon the questions which most deeply interest or most vitally affect humanity is as natural as it is difficult to resist. The desire to see what a book which is talked about is like is doubly hard to overcome when it is so easily excused under the pretense of gaining light on important questions. Time seems to be proving, however, that the amount of noise made over these theory-mongering romances is pretty nearly in adverse ratio to their worth. We are told in Scripture that wisdom calleth in the streets, and no man regardeth, but the opposite seems to be true of the clamors of error. The very vehemence of these books is the quality which secures to them attention; and it is impossible wholly to ignore them, and yet to keep in touch with the time.

It is the more difficult to evade pretentious and noisily worthless writings because of the great ingenuity of the advertising devices which force them upon the attention. The student of genuine literature naturally does not allow himself to be led by these, no matter how persuasive they may be. The man who bases his choice of books upon the advertisements is like him who regulates the health of his family by the advice of a patent-medicine almanac. It is not easy, however, to escape entirely from the influence of advertising. If we have seen a book talked about in print, been confronted with its title on a dazzling poster, if it has been recommended by the chief prize-fighter in the land, or damned by the admiration of Mr. Gladstone, we are any of us inclined to read it, just to see what it is like. The ways by which new publications are insinuated upon the attention are, too, so impalpably effective, so cunningly unexpected, that we take our opinion from them without realizing that we have originated it. The inspiration and stress of which in Greece begot art, bring forth in our day advertising, and no man can wholly escape its influence.

Innumerable are the methods by which authors, whose sole claim to genius is this skill in advertising, keep themselves and their books before the public. Eccentricities of manner and of matter are so varied as to provoke wonder that mental fertility of resource so remarkable should not produce results really great and lasting. Some writers claim to be founders of schools, and talk a good deal about their "modernity," a word which really means stale sensationalism revamped; others insist in season and out of season that they have discovered the only true theory of art, and that literature is only possible upon the lines which they lay down. It is unfortunately to be observed that the theory invariably follows the practice; that they first produce queer books, and then formulate a theory which excuses them. Still others call attention to themselves by a variety of artifices, from walking down Piccadilly mooning over a sunflower to driving through the Bois de Boulogne in brocade coat, rose-pink hat, and cravat of gold-lace, like Barbey d'Aurevilly. No man ever produced good art who worked to advertise himself, and fortunately the day of these charlatans is usually short. I have spoken in another place of the danger of confounding an author and his work; and of course this peril is especially great in the case of writers of our own time. I may add that the parading of authors is a vice especially prevalent in the nineteenth century. Mrs. Leo Hunter advertises herself, and incidentally the celebrities whom she captures, and the publishers not infrequently show a disposition to promote the folly for the sake of their balance-sheet. If Apollo and the Muses returned to earth they would be bidden instantly to one of Mrs. Hunter's Saturday five o'clocks, and a list of the distinguished guests would be in the

Sunday papers. That is what many understand by the encouragement of literature.

Another method of securing notice, which is practiced by not a few latter-day writers, is that of claiming startling originality. Many of the authors who are attempting to take the kingdom of literary distinction by violence lay great stress upon the complete novelty of their views or their emotions. Of these, it is perhaps sufficient to say that the men who are genuine insist that what they say is true, not that they are the first to say it. In all art that is of value the end sought is the work and not the worker. Perhaps most vicious of all these self-advertisers are those who force themselves into notice by thrusting forward whatever the common consent of mankind has hitherto kept concealed. It is chiefly to France that we owe this development of recent literature so-called. If a French writer wishes to be effective, it is apparently his instant instinct to be indecent. The trick is an easy one. It is as if the belle who finds herself a wall-flower at a ball should begin loudly to swear. She would be at once the centre of observation.

Of books of these various classes Max Nordau has made a dismal list in " Degeneration," a book itself discouragingly bulky, discouragingly opinionated, discouragingly prejudiced and illogical, and yet not without much rightness both of perception and intention. He says of the books most popular with that portion of society which is most in evidence, that they diffuse a curious perfume, yielding distinguishable odors of incense, eau de Lubin, and refuse, one or the other preponderating alternately. . . . Books treating of the relations of the sexes, with no matter how little reserve, seem too dully moral. Elegant titillation only begins where normal sexual relations leave off. . . . Ghost-stories are very popular, but they must come on in scientific disguise, as hypnotism, telepathy, or somnambulism. So are marionette plays, in which seemingly naïve but knowing rogues make used-up old ballad dummies babble like babies or idiots. So are esoteric novels in which the author hints that he could say a deal about magic, fakirism, kabbala, astrology, and other white and black arts if he chose. Readers intoxicate themselves in the hazy word-sequences of symbolic poetry. Ibsen dethrones Goethe; Maeterlinck ranks with Shakespeare; Neitzsche is pronounced by German and even French critics to be the leading German writer of the day; the "Kreutzer Sonata" is the Bible of ladies, who are amateurs in love, but bereft of lovers; dainty gentlemen find the street ballads and gaol-bird songs of Jules Jouy, Bruant, MacNab, and Xanroff very *distingué* on account of "the warm sympathy pulsing in them," as the phrase runs; and society persons, whose creed is limited to baccarat and the money market, make pilgrimages to the Oberammergau Passion-Play, and wipe away a tear over Paul Verlaine's invocations to the Virgin.— *Degeneration*, ii.

This is a picture true of only a limited section of modern society, a section, moreover, much smaller in America than abroad. Common sense and a sense of humor save Americans from many of the extravagances to be observed across the ocean. There are too many fools, however, even in this country. To secure immediate success with these readers a writer need do nothing more than to produce erotic eccentricities. There are many intellectually restless persons who suppose themselves to be advancing in culture when they are poring over the fantastic imbecilities of Maeterlinck, or the nerve-rasping unreason of Ibsen; when they are sailing aloft on the hot-air balloons of Tolstoi's extravagant theories, or wallowing in the blackest mud of Parisian slums with Zola. Dull and jaded minds find in these things an excitement, as the jaded palate finds stimulation in the sting of fiery sauces. There are others, too, who believe that these books are great because they are so impressive. The unreflective reader measures the value of a book not by its permanent qualities but by its instantaneous effect, and an instantaneous effect is very apt to be simple sensationalism.

It is not difficult to see the fallacy of these amazing books. A blackguard declaiming profanely and obscenely in a drawing-room can produce in five minutes more sensation than a sage discoursing learnedly, delightfully, and profoundly could cause in years. Because a book makes the reader cringe it by no means follows that the author is a genius. In literature any writer of ordinary cleverness may gain notoriety if he is willing to be eccentric enough, extravagant enough, or indecent enough. An ass braying attracts more attention than an oriole singing. The street musician, scraping a foundling fiddle, vilely out of tune, compels notice; but the master, freeing the ecstasy enchanted in the bosom of a violin of royal lineage, touches and transports. All standards are confounded if notoriety means excellence.

There is a sentence in one of the enticing and stimulating essays of James Russell Lowell which is applicable to these writers who gain reputation by setting on edge the reader's teeth.

> There is no work of genius which has not been the delight of mankind. — *Rousseau and the Sentimentalists.*

Notice: the delight of mankind; not the sensation, the pastime, the amazement, the horror, or the scandal of mankind, — but the delight. This is a wise test by which to try a good deal of the best advertised literature of the present day. Do not ask whether the talked-of book startles, amuses, shocks, or even arouses simply; but inquire, if you care to estimate its literary value, whether it delights.

It is necessary, of course, to understand that Mr. Lowell uses the word here in its broad signification. He means more than the simple pleasure of smooth and sugary things. He means the delight of tragedy as well as of comedy; of "King Lear" and "Othello" as well as of "Midsummer Night's Dream;" but he does not mean the nerve-torture of "Ghosts" or the mental nausea of "L'Assommoir." By delight he means that persuasion which is an essential quality of all genuine art. The writer who makes his readers shrink and quiver may produce a transient sensation. His notoriety is noisily proclaimed by the trumpets of to-day; but the brazen voice of to-morrow will as lustily roar other fleeting successes, and all alike be forgotten in a night.

I insisted in the first of these talks upon the principle that good art is " human and wholesome and sane." We need to keep these characteristics constantly in mind; and to make them practical tests of the literature upon which we feed our minds and our imaginations. We are greatly in need of some sort of an artistic quarantine. Literature should not be the carrier of mental or emotional contagion. A work which swarms with mental and moral microbes should be as ruthlessly disinfected by fire as if it were a garment contaminated with the germs of fever or cholera. It is manifestly impossible that this shall be done, however, in the present state of society; and it follows that each reader must be his own health-board in the choice of books.

The practical question which instantly arises is how one is to know good books from bad until one has read them. How to distinguish between what is worthy of attention and what is ephemeral trash has perplexed many a sincere and earnest student. This is a duty which should devolve largely upon trained critics, but unhappily criticism is not to-day in a condition which makes it reliable or practically of very great assistance where recent publications are concerned. The reader is left to his own judgment in choosing among writings hot from the press. Fortunately the task of discriminating is not impossible. It is even far less difficult than it at first appears. The reader is seldom without a pretty clear idea of the character of notorious books before he touches them. Where the multitude of publications is so great, the very means of advertising which are necessary to bring them into notice show what they are. Even should a man make it a rule to read nothing until he has a definite estimate of its merit, he will find in the end that he has lost little. For any purposes of the cultivation of the mind or the imagination the book which is good to read to-day is good to read to-morrow, so that there is not the haste about reading a real book that there is in getting through the morning paper, which becomes obsolete by noon. When one considers, too, how small a portion of the volumes published it is possible to have time for, and how important it is to make the most of life by having these of the best, one realizes that it is worth while to take a good deal of trouble, and if need be to sacrifice the superficial enjoyment of keeping in the front rank of the mad mob of sensation seekers whose only idea of literary merit is noise and novelty. It is a trivial and silly vanity which is unhappy because somebody — or because everybody — has read new books first.

There is, moreover, nothing more stupid than the attempt to deceive ourselves, — especially if the attempt succeeds. Of all forms of lying this is at once the most demoralizing and the most utterly useless. If we read poor books from puerile or unworthy motives, let us at least be frank about it in our own minds. If we have taken up with unwholesome writers from idle curiosity, or, worse, from prurient hankering after uncleanness, what do we gain by assuring ourselves that we did not know what we were doing, or by pretending that we have unwillingly been following out a line of scientific investigation? Fine theories make but flimsy coverings for unhealthy desires.

Of course this whole matter lies within the domain of individual liberty and individual responsibility. The use or the abuse of reading is determined by each man for himself. To gloat over scorbutic prose and lubricious poetry, to fritter the attention upon the endless repetition of numberless insignificant details, to fix the mind upon phonographic reports of the meaningless conversations of meaningless characters, to lose rational consciousness in the confusion of verbal eccentricities which dazzle by the cunning with which words are prevented from conveying intelligence, — and the writings of to-day afford ample opportunity for doing all of these things! — is within the choice of every reader. It is to be remembered, however, that no excuse evades the consequence. He who wastes life finds himself bankrupt, and there is no redress.

Always it is to be remembered that the classics afford us the means of measuring the worth of what we read. He who pauses to consider a little will see at once something of what is meant by this. He will realize the wide difference there is between familiarity with the permanent literature of the world and acquaintance with the most sensational and widely discussed books of to-day. A man may be a virtuous citizen and a good husband and father, with intelligence in his business and common sense in the affairs of life, and yet be utterly ignorant of how Achilles put the golden tress into the hand of dead Patroclus, or of the stratagem by which Iphigenia saved the life of Orestes at Tauris, or of the love of Palamon and Arcite for Emilie the fair, or of whom Gudrun married and whom she loved, or of how Sancho Panza governed his island, or of the ill-fated loves of Romeo and Juliet, or of the agony of Othello, or of Hamlet, or Lear, or Perdita, or Portia. The knowledge of none of these is necessary to material existence, and it is possible to make a creditable figure in the world without it. Yet we are all conscious that the man who is not aware of these creations which are so much more real than the majority of the personages that stalk puppet-like across the pages of history, has missed something of which the loss makes his life definitely poorer. We cannot but feel the enrichment of mind and feeling which results from our having in classic pages made the acquaintance with these gracious beings and shared their adventures and their emotions. Suppose that the books most noisily lauded to-day were to be tried by the same test. Is a man better for knowing with Zola all the diseased genealogy of the Rougon-Macquart family, morbid, criminal, and foul? Is not the mind cleaner and saner if it has never been opened to the entertainment of Poznyscheff, Hedda Gabler, Dr. Rank, Mademoiselle de Maupin, Oswald Alving, or any of this unclean tribe? It is not that a strong or well-developed man will ignore the crime or the criminals of the world; but it is not necessary to gloat over either. It is not difficult to learn all that it is necessary to know about yellow fever, cholera, or leprosy, without passing days and nights in the pest hospitals.

These unwholesome books, however, are part of the intellectual history of our time. He who would keep abreast of modern thought and of life as it is to-day, we are constantly reminded, must take account of the writers who are most loudly lauded. Goethe has said: "It is in her monstrosities that nature reveals herself;" and the same is measurably true in the intellectual world. The madness, the eccentricity, the indecencies of these books, are so many indications by which certain tendencies of the period betray themselves. It seems to me, however, that this is a consideration to which it is extremely easy to give too much weight. To mistake this noisy and morbid class of books, these self-parading and sensational authors, for the most significant signs of the intellectual condition of the time is like mistaking a drum-major for the general, because the drum-major is most conspicuous and always to the fore, — except in action. The mind is nourished and broadened, moreover, by the study of sanity. It is the place of the physician to concern himself with disease; but as medical treatises are dangerous in the hands of laymen, so are works of morbid psychology in the hands of the ordinary reader.

Fortunately contemporary literature is not confined to books of the unwholesome sort, greatly as these are in evidence. We have a real literature as well as a false one. Time moves so swiftly that we have begun to regard the works of Thackeray and Dickens and Hawthorne, and almost of Browning and Tennyson, as among the classics. They are so, however, by evident merit rather than by age, and have not been in existence long enough to receive the suffrages of generations. The names of these authors remind us how many books have been written in our time which endure triumphantly all tests that have been proposed; books to miss the knowledge of which is to lose the opportunity of making life richer. Certainly we should be emotionally and spiritually poorer without the story of Hester Prynne and Arthur Dimmesdale, between whom the Scarlet Letter glowed balefully; without Hilda in her tower and poor Miriam bereft of her Faun below. To have failed to share the Fezziwigs' ball, or the trial of Mr. Pickwick for breach of promise; to have lived without knowing the inimitable Sam Weller and the juicy Micawbers, the amiable Quilp and the elegant Mrs. Skewton, philanthropic Mrs. Jellyby and airy Harold Skimpole, is to have failed of acquaintances that would have brightened existence; to be ignorant of Becky Sharp and Colonel Newcome, of Arthur Pendennis and George Warrington, of Beatrix and Colonel Esmond, is to have neglected one of the blessings, and not of the lesser blessings either. No man is without a permanent and tangible gain who has comprehendingly read Emerson's "Rhodora," or the "Threnody," or "Days," or "The Problem." Whoever has been sympathetically through the "Idylls of the King" not only experienced a long delight but has gained a fresh ideal; while to have gone to the heart of "The Ring and the Book," — that most colossal *tour-de-force* in all literature, — to have heard the tender confidences of dying Pompilia, the anguished confession of Caponsacchi, the noble soliloquy of the Pope, is to have lived through a spiritual and an emotional experience of worth incalculable. In the age of Thackeray and Dickens, of Hawthorne and Emerson and Tennyson and Browning, we cannot complain that there is any lack of genuine literature.

Nor are we obliged to keep to what seems to some a high and breathless altitude of reading. There are many readers who are of so little natural imagination, or who have cultivated it so little, that it is a conscious and often a fatiguing effort to keep to the mood of these greater authors. Beside these works to the keen enjoyment of which imagination is necessary, there are others which are genuine without being of so high rank. It is certainly on the whole a misfortune that one should be deprived of a knowledge of Mrs. Proudie and the whole clerical circle in which she moved, and especially of Mr. Harding, the delightful "Warden;" he is surely to be pitied who has not read the story of "Silas Marner," who does not feel friendly and intimate with shrewd and epigrammatic Mrs. Poyser, with spiritual Dinah Morris, and with Maggie

Tulliver and her family. No intelligent reader can afford to have passed by in neglect the pleasant sweetness of Longfellow or the wholesome soundness of Whittier, the mystic sensuousness of Rossetti or the voluptuous melodiousness of Swinburne.

It is manifestly impossible to enumerate all the authors who illustrate the richness of the latter half of the nineteenth century; but there are those of the living who cannot be passed in silence. To deal with those who are writing to-day is manifestly difficult, but as I merely claim to cite illustrations no fault can justly be found with omissions. Naturally Meredith and Hardy come first to mind. He who has read that exquisite chapter in "The Ordeal of Richard Feverel" which tells of the meeting of Richard and Lucy in the meadows by the river has in memory a gracious possession for the rest of his days. Who can recall from "The Return of the Native" the noonday visit of Mrs. Yeobright to the house of her son and her journey to death back over Egdon Heath, without a heart-deep thrill? What sympathetic reader fails to recognize that he is mentally and imaginatively richer for the honest little reddle-man, Diggory Venn, for sturdy Gabriel Oak, for the delightful clowns of "Under the Greenwood Tree" and "Far from the Madding Crowd," or for ill-starred Tess when on that dewy morning she had the misfortune to touch the caddish heart of Angel Clare? To have failed to read and to reread Stevenson, — for one thinks of Stevenson as still of the living, — to have passed Kipling by, is to have neglected one of the blessings of the time.

It may be that I have seemed to imply by the examples I have chosen that the literature of continental Europe is to be shunned. Naturally in addressing English-speaking folk one selects examples when possible from literature in that tongue; and I have alluded to books in other languages only when they brought out more strikingly than do English books a particular point. It is needless to say that in these cosmopolitan days no one can afford to neglect the riches of other nations in contemporary literature. It is difficult to resist the temptation to make lists, to speak of the men who in France with Guy de Maupassant at their head have developed so great a mastery of style; one would gladly dwell on the genius of Turgenieff, perhaps the one writer who excuses the modern craze for Russian books; or of Sienkiewicz, who has only Dumas *père* to dispute his place as first romancer of the world; and so on for other writers of other lands and tongues. It is unnecessary, however, to multiply examples, and here there is no attempt to speak exhaustively even of English literature.

The thing to be kept in mind is that it is our good fortune to live in the century which in the whole course of English literature is outranked by the brilliant Elizabethan period only. It is surely worth while to attempt to prove ourselves worthy of that which the gods have graciously given us. Men sigh for the good day that is gone, and imagine that had they lived then they would have made their lives correspondingly rich to match the splendors of an age now famous. We live in a time destined to go down to the centuries not unrenowned for literary achievement; it is for us to prove ourselves appreciative and worthy of this time.

XIV

FICTION

PROBABLY the oldest passion of the race which can lay any claim to connection with the intellect is the love of stories. The most ancient examples of literature which have been preserved are largely in the form of narratives. As soon as man has so far conquered the art of speech as to get beyond the simplest statements, he may be supposed to begin instinctively to relate incidents, to tell rudimentary tales, and to put into words the story of events which have happened, or which might have happened.

The interest which every human being takes in the things which may befall his fellows underlies this universal fondness; and the man who does not love a story must be devoid of normal human sympathy with his kind. It is hardly necessary, at this late day, to point out the strong hold upon the sympathies of his fellows which the story-teller has had from the dawn of civilization. The mind easily pictures the gaunt reciters who, in savage tribes, repeat from generation to generation the stories and myths handed orally from father to son; or the professional narrators of the Orient who repeat gorgeously colored legends and fantastic adventures in the gate or the market. Perhaps, too, the mention of the subject of this talk brings from the past the homely, kindly figure of the nurse who made our childish eyes grow large, and our little hearts go trippingly in the days of pinafores and fairy-lore — the blessed days when " once upon a time " was the open sesame to all delights. The responsiveness of human beings to story-telling the world over unites all mankind as in a bond of common sympathy.

What old-fashioned theologians seemed to find an inexhaustible pleasure in calling " the natural man " has always been strongly inclined to turn in his reading to narratives in preference to what our grandparents primly designated as " improving works." In any library the bindings of the novels are sure to be worn, while the sober backs of treatises upon manners, or morals, or philosophy, or even science, remain almost as fresh as when they left the bindery. Each reader in his own grade selects the sort of tale which most appeals to him; and while the range is wide, the principle of selection is not so greatly varied. The shop-girl gloats over " The Earl's Bride; or, The Heiress of Plantagenet Park." The school-miss in the street-car smiles contemptuously as she sees this title, and complacently opens the volume of the " Duchess " or of Rhoda Broughton which is the delight of her own soul. The advanced young woman of society has only contempt for such trash, and accompanies her chocolate caramels with the perusal of " The Yellow Aster," or the " Green

Carnation," while her mother, very likely, reads the felicitous foulness of some Frenchman. Those readers who have a sane and wholesome taste, properly cultivated, take their pleasure in really good novels or stories; but the fondness for narrative of some sort is universal.

It would be manifestly unfair to imply that there is never a natural inclination for what is known as "solid reading," but such a taste is exceptional rather than general. Certainly a person who cared only for stories could not be looked upon as having advanced far in intellectual development; but appreciation for other forms of literature is rather the effect of cultivation than the result of natural tendencies. Most of us have had periods in which we have endeavored to persuade ourselves that we were of the intellectual elect, and that however circumstances had been against us, we did in our inmost souls pant for philosophy and yearn for abstract wisdom. We are all apt to assure ourselves that if we might, we should devote our days to the study of science and our nights to mastering the deepest secrets of metaphysics. We declare to ourselves that we have not time; that just now we are wofully overworked, but that in some golden, although unfortunately indeterminate future, for which we assure ourselves most solemnly that we long passionately, we shall pore over tremendous tomes of philosophical thought as the bee grapples itself to a honey-full clover-blossom. It is all humbug; and, what is more, we know that it is humbug. We do not, as a rule, relish the effort of comprehending and assimilating profoundly thoughtful literature, and it is generally more easy to read fiction in a slipshod way than it is to glide with any amusement over intellectual work. The intense strain of the age of course increases this tendency to light reading; but in any age the only books of which practically everybody who reads at all is fond are the story-books.

It has been from time to time the habit of busy idlers to fall into excited and often acrimonious discussion in regard to this general love for stories. Many have held that it is an instinct of a fallen and unregenerate nature, and that it is to be checked at any cost. It is not so long since certain most respectable and influential religious sects set the face steadfastly against novels; and you may remember as an instance that when George Eliot was a young woman she regarded novel-reading as a wicked amusement. There is to-day a more rational state of feeling. It is seen that it is better to accept the instincts of human nature, and endeavor to work through them than to engage in the well-nigh hopeless task of attempting to eradicate them. To-day we are coming to recognize the cunning of the East in inculcating wisdom in fables and the profound lesson of the statement in the Gospels: " Without a parable spake He not unto them."

Much of the distrust which has been in the' past felt in regard to fiction has arisen from a narrow and uncomprehending idea of its nature. Formalists have conceived that the relating of things which never occurred — which indeed it was often impossible should occur, — is a violation of truth. The fundamental ground of most of the objections which moralists have made to fiction has been the assumption that fiction is false. Of certain kinds of fiction this is of course true enough, but of fiction which comes within the range of literature it is conspicuously incorrect.

Fiction is literature which is false to the letter that it may be true to the spirit. It is unfettered by narrow actualities of form, because it has to express the higher actualities of emotion. It uses incident and character as mere language. It is as unfair to object to the incidents of a great novel that they are untrue, as it would be to say that the letters of a word are untrue. There is no question of truth or untruth beyond the question whether the symbols express that which they are intended to convey. The letters are set down to impart to the intelligence of the reader the idea of a given word; the incidents of a novel are used to embody a truth of human nature and life. Truth is here the verity of the thing conveyed. In a narrow and literal sense Hamlet and Othello and Colonel Newcome and Becky Sharp are untrue. They never existed in the flesh. They have lived, however, in the higher and more vital sense that they have been part of the imagination of a master. They are true in that they express the truth. It is a dull misunderstanding of the value of things to call that book untrue which deals with fictitious characters wisely, yet to hold as verity that which records actual events stolidly and unappreciatively. The history may be false from beginning to end and the fiction true. Fiction which is worthy of consideration under the name of literature is the truest prose in the world; and I believe that it is not without an instinctive recognition of this fact that mankind has so generally taken it to its heart.

The value of at least certain works of fiction has come to be generally recognized by the intellectual world. There are some novels which it is taken for granted that every person of education has read. Whoever makes the smallest pretense of culture must, for instance, be at least tolerably familiar with Scott, Thackeray, Dickens, and Hawthorne; while he will find it difficult to hold the respect of cultivated men unless he is also acquainted with Miss Austen, George Eliot, and Charlotte Brontë, with Dumas *père*, Balzac, and Victor Hugo, and with the works of leading living writers of romance. "Don Quixote" is as truly a necessary part of a liberal education as is the multiplication table; and it would not be difficult to extend the list of novels which it is assumed as a matter of course that persons of cultivation know familiarly.

Nor is it only the works of the greater writers of imaginative narration which have secured a general recognition. If it is not held that it is essential for an educated man to have read Trollope, Charles Reade, Kingsley, or Miss Mulock, for example, it is at least recognized that one had better have gained an acquaintance with these and similar writers. Traill, the English critic, speaks warmly of the books which while falling below the first rank are yet richly worth attention. He says with justice: —

The world can never estimate the debt that it owes to second-class literature. Yet it is basely afraid to acknowledge the debt, hypocritically desiring to convey the impression that such literature comes to it in spite of protest, calling off its attention from the great productions.

It is true enough that there is a good deal of foolish pretense in regard to our genuine taste in reading, but in actual practice most persons do in the long run read chiefly what they really enjoy. It is also true that there are more readers who are capable of appreciating the novels of the second grade than there are those who are in sympathy with fiction of the first. The thing for each individual reader is to see to it that he is honest in this matter with himself, and that he gives attention to the best that he can like rather than to the poorest.

Even those who accept the fact that cultivated persons will read novels, and those who go so far as to appreciate that it is a distinct gain to the intellectual life, are, however, very apt to be troubled by the dangers of over-indulgence in this sort of literature. It has been said and repeated innumerable times that the excessive reading of novels is mentally debilitating and even debauching. This is certainly true. So is it true that there is great mental danger in the excessive reading of philosophy or theology, or the excessive eating of bread, or the excessive doing of any other thing. The favorite figure in connection with fiction has been to compare it to opium-eating or to dram-drinking; and the moral usually drawn is that the novel-reader is in imminent danger of intellectual dissoluteness or even of what might be called the delirium tremens of the imagination. I should not be honest if I pretended to have a great deal of patience with most that is said in this line The exclusive use of fiction as mental food is of course unwise, and the fact is so patent that it is hardly worth while to waste words in repeating it. When I said a moment ago that there is danger in the eating of bread if it is carried to excess I indicated what seems to me to be the truth in this matter. If one reads good and wholesome fiction, I believe that the natural instincts of the healthy mind may be trusted to settle the question of how much shall be read. If the fiction is unhealthy, morbid, or false, any of it is bad. If it is good, if it calls into play a healthy imagination, there is very little danger that too much of it will be taken. When there is complaint that a girl or a boy is injuring the mind by too exclusive a devotion to novels, I believe that it generally means, if the facts of the case were understood, that the mind of the reader is in an unwholesome condition, and that this excessive devotion to fiction is a symptom rather than a disease. When the girl coughs, it is not the cough that is the trouble; this is only a symptom of the irritation of membranes; and I believe that much the same is the case with extravagant novel-readers.

Of course this view of the matter will not commend itself to everybody. It is hard for us to shake off the impression of all the countless homilies which have been composed against novel-reading; and we are by no means free from the poison of the ascetic idea that anything to which mankind takes naturally and with pleasure cannot really be good in itself. I hope, however, that it will not appear to you unreasonable when I say that it seems to me far better to insist upon proper methods of reading and upon the selection of books which are genuine literature than to wage unavailing war against the natural love of stories which is to be found in every normal and wholesome human being. If I could be assured that a boy or a girl read only good novels and read them appreciatively and sympathetically, I should never trouble myself to inquire how many he or she read. I should be hopefully patient even if there was apparently a neglect of history and philosophy. I should be confident that it is impossible that the proper reading of good fiction should not in the end both prove beneficial in itself and lead the mind to whatever is good in other departments of literature. I am not pleading for the indiscriminating indulgence in doubtful stories. I do not believe that girls are brought to fine and well-developed womanhood by an exclusive devotion to the chocolate-caramel-and-pickled-lime sort of novels. I do not hold that boys come to nobility and manliness through the influence of sensational tales wherein blood-boultered bandits reduce to infinitesimal powder every commandment of the decalogue. I do, however, thoroughly believe that sound and imaginative fiction is as natural and as wholesome for growing minds as is the air of the seashore or the mountains for growing bodies.

The fact is of especial importance as applied to the education of children. A healthy child is instinctively in the position of a learner. He is unconsciously full of deep wonderment concerning this world in which he finds himself, and concerning this mysterious thing called life in which he has a share. His mind is eager to receive, but it is entirely free from any affectation. A child accepts what appeals to him directly, and he is without scruple in neglecting what does not interest him. He learns only by slow degrees that knowledge may have value and interest from its remote bearings; and in dealing with him in the earlier stages of mental development there is no other means so sure and effective as story-telling. It is here that a child finds the specific and the concrete while he is still too immature to be moved by the general and the abstract.

It is "to cater to this universal taste," the circulars of the publishers assure us, that so-called "juvenile literature" was invented. I do not wish to be extravagant, but it does seem to me that modern juvenile literature has blighted the rising generation as rust blights a field of wheat. The holiday counters are piled high with hastily written, superficial, often inaccurate, and, what is most important of all, unimaginative books. The nursery of to-day is littered with worthless volumes, and the child halfway through school has already outlived a dozen varieties of books for the young.

A good many of these works are as full of information as a sugar-coated pill is of drugs. Thirst for practical information is one of the extravagances of the age. Parents to-day make their children to pass through tortures in the service of what they call "practical knowledge" as the unnatural parents of old made their offspring to pass through the fires of Moloch. We are all apt to lose sight of the fact that wisdom is not what a man knows but what he is. The important thing is not what we drill into our children, but what we drill them into. There are times when it is the most profound moral duty of a parent to substitute Grimm's fairy stories for text-books, and to devote the whole stress of educational effort to the developing of the child's imagination. I am not at all sure that it is not of more importance to see to it that a child — and especially a boy — is familiar with "the land east of the sun and west of the moon" than to stuff his brain with the geographical details of the wilds of Asia, Africa, or the isles of the far seas. I am sure that he is better off from knowing about Sindbad and Ali Baba than for being able to extract a cube root. I do not wish to be understood as speaking against the imparting of practical information, although I must say that I think that the distinction between what is really practical and

what is not seems to me to be somewhat confused
in these days. I simply mean that just now there
is need of enforcing the value of the imaginative
side of education. No accumulation of facts can
compensate for the narrowing of the growing mind;
and indeed facts are not to be really grasped and
assimilated without the development of the realizing — the imaginative — faculty.

It is even more important for children than for
adults that their reading shall be imaginative.
The only way to protect them against worthless
books is to give them a decided taste for what is
good. It is only after children have been debauched
by vapid or sensational books that they come to
delight in rubbish. It is easier in the first place
to interest them in real literature than in shams.
The thing is to take the trouble to see to it that
what they read is fine. The most common error
in this connection is to suppose that children need
an especial sort of literature different from that
suited to adults. As far, certainly, as serious education is concerned, there is neither adult literature
nor juvenile literature; there is simply literature.
Speaking broadly, the literature best for grown
persons is the literature best for children. The
limitations of youth have, and should have, the
same effects in literature as in life. They restrict
the comprehension and appreciation of the facts
of life; and equally they set a bound to the comprehension and appreciation of what is read. The
impressions which a child gets from either are not
those of his elders. The important thing is that

what the growing mind receives shall be vital and wholesome. It is less unfortunate for the child to mistake what is genuine than to receive as true what is really false. We all commit errors in the conclusions which we draw from life; and so will it be with children and books. Books which are wise and sane, however, will in time correct the misconceptions they beget, as life in time makes clear the mistakes which life has produced.

The whole philosophy of reading for children is pretty well summed up by implication in the often quoted passage in which Charles Lamb describes under the disguise of Bridget Elia, the youthful experience of his sister Mary : —

> She was tumbled early, by accident or design, into a spacious closet of good old English reading, without much selection or prohibition, and browsed at will upon that fair and wholesome pasturage. Had I twenty girls, they should be brought up exactly in this fashion. — *Mackery End.*

Fiction — to return to the immediate subject of this talk — is only a part of a child's education, but it is a most essential part; and it is of the greatest importance that the fiction given to a young reader be noble ; that it be true to the essentials of life, as it can be true only if it is informed by a keen and sane imagination. Children should be fed on the genuine and sound folk-tales like those collected by the brothers Grimm ; the tales of Hans Christian Andersen, of Asbjörnsen, of Laboulaye, and of that delightful old lady, the Countess d'Aulnoy ; the fine and robust " Morte d'Arthur " of Malory; the more modern classics, "Robinson Crusoe" and "Gulliver." Then there are Hawthorne's "Tanglewood Tales" and the "Wonder-Book," "Treasure Island" and "Kidnapped," "Uncle Remus," and the "Jungle Books." It may be claimed that these are "juvenile" literature; but I have named nothing of which I, at least, am not as fond now as in my youth, and I have yet to discover that adults find lack of interest in good books even of fairy stories. What has been said against juvenile literature has been intended against the innumerable works mustered under that name which are not literature at all. Wonder lore is as normal food for old as for young, and there is no more propriety in confining it to children than there is in limiting the use of bread and butter to the inhabitants of the nursery.

It is neither possible nor wise to attempt here a catalogue of books especially adapted to children. I should myself put Spenser high in the list, and very likely include others which common custom does not regard as well adapted to the young. These, of course, are books to be read to the child, not that he at first can be expected to go pleasurably through alone. Prominent among them I would insist first, last, and always upon Shakespeare. If it were practically possible to confine the reading of a child to Shakespeare and the Bible, the whole question would be well and wisely settled. Since this cannot be, it is at least essential that a child be given both as soon as he can be interested in them, — and it is equally important that he be given neither until they do attract him. He is to be guided and aided, but there cannot be a more rich and noble introduction to fiction than through the inspired pages of Shakespeare, and the child who has been well grounded in the greatest of poets is not likely ever to go very widely astray in his reading.

XV

FICTION AND LIFE

THE reading of fiction has come to have an important and well recognized place in modern life. However strong may be the expression of disapprobation against certain individual books, no one in these days attempts to deny the value of imaginative literature in the development of mind and the formation of character; yet so strong is the Puritan strain in the blood of the English race that there is still a good deal of lingering ascetic disapproval of novels.

It must be remembered in this connection that there are novels and novels. The objections which have from time to time been heaped upon fiction in general are more than deserved by fiction in particular; and that, too, by the fiction most in evidence. The books least worthy are for the most part precisely those which in their brief day are most likely to excite comment. That the flaming scarlet toadstools which irresistibly attract the eye in the forest are viciously poisonous does not, however, alter the fact that mushrooms are at once delicious and nutritious. It is no more logical to condemn all fiction on account of the worthlessness or hurtfulness of bad books than it would be to denounce all food because things have often been eaten which are dangerously unwholesome.

The great value of fiction as a means of intellectual and of moral training lies in the fact that man is actually and vitally taught nothing of importance save by that which really touches his feelings. Advice appeals to the intellect, and experience to the emotions. What has been didactically told to us is at best a surface treatment, while what we have felt is an inward modification of what we are. We approve of advice, and we act according to experience. Often when we have decided upon one course of life or action, the inner self which is the concrete result of our temperament and our experiences goes quietly forward in a path entirely different. What we have resolved seldom comes to pass unless it is sustained by what we have felt. For centuries has man been defining himself as a being that reasons while he has been living as a being that feels.

The sure hold of fiction upon mankind depends upon the fact that it enables the reader to gain experience vicariously. Seriously and sympathetically to read a story which is true to life is to live through an emotional experience. How vivid this emotion is will manifestly depend upon the imaginative sympathy with which one reads. The young man who has appreciatively entered into the life of Arthur Pendennis will hardly find that he is able to go through the world in a spirit of dandified self-complaisance without a restraining consciousness that such an attitude toward life is most absurd folly. A man of confirmed worldliness is perhaps not to be turned from his selfish and ignoble living by studying the history of Major Pendennis, to read about whom is not unlike drinking dry and rare old Madeira; yet it is scarcely to be doubted that an appreciation of the figure cut by the old beau, fluttering over the flowers of youth like a preserved butterfly poised on a wire, must tend to lead a man to a different career. No reader can have felt imaginatively the passionate spiritual struggles of Arthur Dimmesdale without being thereafter more sensitive to good influences and less tolerant of self-deception and concealed sin. These are the more obvious examples. The experiences which one gains from good fiction go much farther and deeper. They extend into those most intangible yet most real regions where even the metaphysician, the psychologist, and the maker of definitions have not yet been able to penetrate; those dim, mysterious tracts of the mind which are still to us hardly better known than the unexplored mid-countries of Asia or Africa.

As a means of accomplishing a desired end didactic literature is probably the most futile of all the unavailing attempts of mankind. In the days when ringlets and pantalets were in fashion, when small boys wore frilled collars and asked only improving questions, when the most delirious literary dissipation of which the youthful fancy could conceive was a Rollo book or a prim tale by Maria Edgeworth, it was generally believed that moral precepts and wise maxims had a prodigious influence upon the young. It was held possible to mould the rising generation by putting one of the sentences of Solomon at the head of a copy-book page, and to make a permanent impression upon the spirit by saws and sermons. If this were ever true, it is certainly not true now. If sermon or saw has touched the imagination of the hearer, it has had some effect which will be lasting; and this the saw does oftener than the sermon, the proverb than the precept. If it has won only an intellectual assent, there is small ground for supposing that it will bring about any alteration which will be permanent and effective.

Taking into account these considerations, one might sum up the whole matter somewhat in this way: To read fiction is certainly a pleasure; it is to be looked upon as no less important a means of intellectual development; while in the cultivation of the moral and spiritual sense the proper use of fiction is one of the most effectual and essential agencies to-day within the reach of men. In other words the proper reading of fiction is, from the standpoint of pleasure, of intellectual development, or of moral growth, neither more nor less than a distinct and imperative duty.

I have been careful to say, "the proper reading of fiction." Whatever strictures may be laid upon careless readers in general may perhaps be quadrupled when applied to bad reading of novels. It is the duty of nobody to read worthless fiction; and it is a species of moral iniquity to read good novels carelessly, flippantly, or superficially. There is small literary or intellectual hope for those whom Henry James describes as "people who read novels as an exercise in skipping." There are two tests by which the novel-reader is to be tried: What sort of fiction does he read, and how does he read it? If the answers to these questions are satisfactory, the whole matter is settled.

Of course it is of the first importance that the reader think for himself; that he form his own opinions, and have his own appreciations. Small minds are like weak galvanic cells; one alone is not strong enough to generate a sensible current; they must be grouped to produce an appreciable result. One has no opinion; while to accomplish anything approaching a sensation a whole circle is required. It takes an entire community of such intellects to get up a feeling, and of course the feeling when aroused is shared in common. There are plenty of pretentious readers of all the latest notorious novels who have as small an individual share in whatever emotion the book excites as a Turkish wife has in the multifariously directed affections of her husband. It is impossible not to see the shallowness, the pretense, and the intellectual demoralization of these readers; and it is equally idle to deny the worthlessness of the books in which they delight.

What, then, is to be learned from fiction, that so much stress is to be laid upon the necessity of making it a part of our intellectual and moral education? The answer has in part at least been so often given that it seems almost superfluous to repeat it. The more direct lessons of the novel are so evident as scarcely to call for enumeration. Nobody needs at this late day to be told how much may be learned from fiction of the customs of different grades of society, of the ways and habits of all sorts and conditions of men, and of the even more fascinating if not actually more vitally important manners and morals of all sorts and conditions of women. Every reader knows how much may be learned from stories of the facts of human relations and of social existence, — facts which one accumulates but slowly by actual experience, while yet a knowledge of them is of so great importance for the full appreciation and the proper employment and enjoyment of life.

Civilization is essentially an agreement upon conventions. It is the tacit acceptance of conditions and concessions. It is conceded that if human beings are to live together it is necessary that there must be mutual agreement, and as civilization progresses this is extended to all departments and details of life. What is called etiquette, for instance, is one variety of social agreement into which men have entered for convenience and comfort in living together. What is called good breeding is but the manifestation of a generous desire to observe all those human regulations by which the lives of others may be rendered more happy. These concessions and conventions are not natural. A man may be born with the spirit of good breeding, but he must learn its methods. Nature may bestow the inclination to do what is wisest and best in human relations, but the forms and processes of social life and of all human intercourse must be acquired. It is one of the functions of fiction to instruct in all this knowledge; and only he who is unacquainted with life will account such an office trivial.

Intimate familiarity with the inner characteristics of humanity, and knowledge of the experiences and the nature of mankind, are a still more important gain from fiction. Almost unconsciously the intelligent novel-reader grows in the comprehension of what men are and of what they may be. This art makes the reader a sharer in those moments when sensation is at its highest, emotion at its keenest. It brings into the life which is outwardly quiet and uneventful, into the mind which has few actual experiences to stir it to its deeps, the splendid exhilaration of existence at its best. The pulse left dull by a colorless life throbs and tingles over the pages of a vivid romance; the heart denied contact with actualities which would awaken it beats hotly with the fictitious passion made real by the imagination; so that life becomes forever richer and more full of meaning.

In one way it is possible to gain from these imaginative experiences a knowledge of life more accurate than that which comes from life itself. It is possible to judge, to examine, to weigh, to estimate the emotions which are enjoyed æsthetically; whereas emotions arising from real events benumb all critical faculties by their stinging personal quality. He who has never shared actual emotional experiences has never lived, it is true; but he who has not shared æsthetic emotions has never understood.

What should be the character of fiction is pretty accurately indicated by what has been said of the part which fiction should play in human development. Here, as in all literature, men are less influenced by the appeal to the reason than by the appeal to the feelings. The novelist who has a strong and lasting influence is not he who instructs men directly, but he who moves men. This is instruction in its higher sense. The guidance of life must come from the reason; equally, however, must the impulse of life come from the emotions. The man who is ruled by reason alone is but a curious mechanical toy which mimics the movements of life without being really alive.

This prime necessity of touching and moving the reader determines one of the most important points of difference between literature and science. It forces the story-teller to modify, to select, and to change if need be the facts of life, in order to produce an impression of truth. Out of the multifarious details of existence the author must select the significant; out of the real deduce the possibility which shall commend itself to the reader as verity.

Above everything else is an artist who is worthy of the name truthful in his art. He never permits himself to set down anything which is not a verity to his imagination, or which fails to be consistent with the conditions of human existence. He realizes that fiction in which a knowledge of the outward shell and the accidents of life is made the chief object cannot be permanent and cannot be vitally effective. The novelist is not called upon to paint life, but to interpret life. It is his privilege to be an artist ; and an artist is one who sees through apparent truth to actual verity. It is his first and most essential duty to arouse the inner being, and to this necessity he must be ready to sacrifice literal fact. Until the imagination is awake, art cannot even begin to do its work. It is true that there may be a good deal of pleasant story-telling which but lightly touches the fancy and does not reach deeper. It is often harmless enough; but it is as idle to expect from this any keen or lasting pleasure, and still more any mental experience of enduring significance, as it would be to expect to warm Nova Zembla with a bonfire. What for the moment tickles the fancy goes with the moment, and leaves little trace ; what touches the imagination becomes a fact of life.

Macaulay, in his extraordinarily wrong-headed essay on Milton, has explicitly stated a very widespread heresy when he says : —

> We cannot unite the incompatible advantages of reality and deception, the clear discernment of truth and the exquisite enjoyment of fiction.

This is the ground generally held by unimaginative men. Macaulay had many good gifts and graces, but his warmest admirers would hardly include among them a greatly endowed or vigorously developed imagination. If one cannot unite the advantages of reality and deception, if he cannot join clear discernment of truth to the exquisite enjoyment of fiction, it is because he fails of all just and adequate comprehension of literature. To call fiction deception is simply to fail to understand that real truth may be independent of apparent truth. It would from the point of view of this sentence of Macaulay's be competent to open the Gospels and call the parable of the sower a falsehood because there is no probability that it referred to any particular incident. The stupidity of criticism of fiction which begins with the assumption that it is not true is not unlike that of an endeavor to swallow a chestnut burr and the consequent declaration that the nut is uneatable. If one is not clever enough to get beneath the husk, his opinion is surely not of great value.

In order to enjoy a novel, it is certainly not necessary to believe it in a literal sense. No sane man supposes that Don Quixote ever did or ever could exist. To the intellect the book is little more than a farrago of impossible absurdities. The imagination perceives that it is true to the fundamental essentials of human nature, and understands that the book is true in a sense higher than that of mere literal verity. It is the cultivated man who has the keenest sense of reality, and yet only to the cultivated man is possible the exquisite enjoyment of "Esmond," of "Les Misérables," "The Scarlet Letter," "The Return of the Native," or "The Ordeal of Richard Feverel." So far from being incompatible, the clear discernment of truth and the exquisite enjoyment of fiction are inseparable.

An artist who is worthy of the name is above all else truthful in his art. He never permits himself to set down anything which he does not feel to be true. It is with a truth higher than a literal accuracy, however, that he is concerned. His perception is the servant of his imagination. He observes and he uses the outward facts of life as a means of conveying its inner meanings. It is this that makes him an artist. The excuse for his claiming the attention of the world is that in virtue of his imagination he is gifted with an insight keener and more penetrating than that of his fellows; and his enduring influence depends upon the extent to which he justifies this claim.

With the novel of trifles it is difficult to have any patience whatever. The so-called Realistic story collects insignificant nothings about a slender thread of plot as a filament of cobweb gathers dust in a barn. The cobweb seems to me on the whole the more valuable, since at least it has the benefit of the old wives' theory that it is good to check bleeding. It is a more noble office to be wrapped about a cut finger than to muffle a benumbed mind.

One question which the great mass of novel-readers who are also students of literature are interested to have answered is, How far is it well to read fiction for simple amusement? With this inquiry, too, goes the kindred one whether it is well or ill to relax the mind over light tales of the sort sometimes spoken of as "summer reading." To this it is impossible to give a categorical reply. It is like the question how often and for how long it is wise to sit down to rest while climbing a hill. It depends upon the traveler, and no one else can determine a point which is to be decided by feelings and conditions known alone to him. It is hardly possible and it is not wise to read always with exalted aims. Whatever you might be advised by me or by any other, you would be foolish not to make of fiction a means of grateful relaxation as well as a help in mental growth. Always it is important to remember, however, that there is a wide difference in the ultimate result, according as a person reads for diversion the best that will entertain him or the worst. It is a matter of the greatest moment that our amusements shall not be allowed to debauch our taste. It is necessary to have some standard even in the choice of the most foamy fiction, served like a sherbet on a hot summer afternoon. One does not read vulgar and empty books, even for simple amusement, without an effect upon his own mind. The Chinese are said to have matches in which cockroaches are pitted against each other to fight for the amusement of the oblique-eyed heathen. To be thus ignoble in their very sports indicates a peculiar degradation and poverty of spirit; and there are certain novels so much in the same line that it is difficult to think of their being read without seeing in fancy a group of pig-tailed Celestials hanging breathlessly over a bowl in which struggle the disgusting little insect combatants. To give the mind up to this sort of reading is not to be commended in anybody.

Fortunately we are in this day provided with a great deal of light fiction which is sound and wholesome and genuine as far as it goes. Some of it even goes far in the way of being imaginative and good. As examples — not at all as a list — may be named Blackmore, Crawford, Stanley Weyman, Anthony Hope, or the numerous writers of admirable short stories, Cable, Miss Jewett, Miss Wilkins, J. M. Barrie, Ian Maclaren, or Thomas Nelson Page. All these and others may be read for simple entertainment, and all are worth reading for some more or less strongly marked quality of permanent worth. There are plenty of writers, too, like William Black and Clark Russell and Conan Doyle, concerning the lasting value of whose stories there might easily be a question, yet who do often contrive to be healthily amusing, and who furnish the means of creating a pleasant and restful vacuity in lives otherwise too full. Every reader must make his own choice, and determine for himself how much picnicking he will do on his way up the hill of life. If he is wise he will contrive to find his entertainment chiefly in books which besides being amusing have genuine value; and he will at least see to it that his intellectual dissipations shall be with the better of such books as will amuse him and not with the poorer.

The mention of the short story brings to mind the great part which this form of fiction plays today. The restlessness of the age and the fostering influence of the magazines have united to develop the short story, and it has become one of the most marked of the literary features of the time. It has the advantage of being easily handled and comprehended as a whole, but it lessens the power of seizing in their entirety works which are greater. It tends rather to increase than to diminish mental restlessness, and the lover of short stories will do well not to let any considerable length of time go by without reading some long and far-reaching novel by way of corrective. Another consequence of the wide popularity of the short story is that we have nowadays so few additions to that delightful company of fictitious yet most admirably real personages whose acquaintance the reader makes in longer tales. The delight of knowing these characters is not only one of the most attractive joys of novel-reading, but it is one which helps greatly to brighten life and enhance friendship. Few things add more to the sympathy of comradeship than a community of friends in the enchanted realms of the imagination. Strangers in the flesh become instantly conscious of an intimacy in spirit when they discover a common love for some character in fiction. Two men may be strangers, with no common acquaintances in the flesh, but if they discover that both admire Elizabeth Bennet, or Lizzie Hexam, or Laura Bell, or Ethel Newcome; that both are familiar friends with Pendennis, or Warrington, or Harry Richmond, or Mulvaney, or Alan Breck, or Mowgli, or Zagloba; or belong to the brave brotherhood of D'Artagnan, Athos, Porthos, and Aramis, they have a community of sympathy which brings them very close together.

It is seldom and indeed almost never that the short story gives to the reader this sense of knowing familiarly its characters. If there be a series, as in Kipling's "Jungle Book" or Maclaren's tales, where the same actors appear again and again, of course the effect may be in this respect the same as that of a novel; but cases of this sort are not common. All the aged women of Miss Wilkins' stories, for instance, are apt in the memory either to blend into one composite photograph of the New England old woman, or to stand remotely, not as persons that we know, but rather as types about which we know. The genuine novel-reader will realize that this consideration is really one of no inconsiderable weight; and it is one which becomes more and more pressing with the increase of the influence of the short story.

This consideration is the more important from the fact that novels in which the reader is able to identify himself with the characters are by far the most effective, because thus is he removed from the realities which surround him, and for the time being freed from whatever would hamper his imagination. That which in real life he would be, but may not, he may in fiction blissfully and expandingly realize. The innate sense of justice — not, perhaps, unseconded by the innate vanity; we are all of us human! — demands that human possibilities shall be realized, and in the story in which the reader merges his personality in that of some actor, all this is accomplished. In actual outward experience life justifies itself but rarely; to most men its justification is reached only by the aid of the imagination, and it is largely by the aid of literature that the imagination works. Even more true is this of the other sex. Much that men learn from life women must learn from books; so that to women fiction is the primer of life as well as the textbook of the imagination. By the novels he reads the man gives evidence of his imaginative development; the woman of her intellectual existence.

Fiction should be delightful, absorbing, and above all inspiring. Genuine art may sadden, but it cannot depress; it may bring a fresh sense of the anguish of humanity, but it must from its very nature join with this the consolation of an ideal. The tragedy of human life is in art held to be the source of new courage, of nobler aspiration, because it gives grander opportunities for human emotion to vindicate its superiority to all disasters, all terrors, all woe. The reader does not leave the great tragedies with a soured mind or a pessimistic disbelief in life. "Lear," "Othello," "Romeo and Juliet," tragic as they are, leave him quivering with sympathy but not with bitterness. The inspiration of the thought of love triumphant over death, of moral grandeur unsubdued by the worst that fate can do, lifts the mind above the disaster. One puts down "The Kreutzer Sonata" with the very flesh creeping with disgust at human existence; the same sin is treated no less tragically in "The Scarlet Letter," yet the reader is left with an inspiration and a nobler feeling toward life. The attitude of art is in its essence hopeful, and the work of the pessimist must therefore fail, even though it be informed with all the cleverness and the witchery of genius.

It is, I believe, from something akin to a remote and perhaps half-conscious perception of this principle that readers in general desire that a novel shall end pleasantly. The popular sentiment in favor of a "happy ending" is by no means so entirely wrong or so utterly Philistine as it is the fashion in these super-æsthetical days to assume. The trick of a doleful conclusion has masqued and paraded as a sure proof of artistic inspiration when it is nothing of the kind. Unhappy endings may be more common than happy ones in life, although even that proposition is by no means proved; they seem so from the human habit of marking the disagreeables and letting pleasant things go unnoted. Writers of a certain school have assumed from this that they were keeping more close to life if they left the reader at the close of a story in a state of darkest melancholy; and they have made much parade of the claim that this is not only more true to fact, but more artistic. There is no reason for such an assumption. The artistic climax of a tale is that which grows out of the story by compelling necessity. There are many narrations, of course, which would become essentially false if made to end gladly. When the ingenious Frenchman rewrote the last act of "Hamlet," marrying off the Prince and dismissing him with Ophelia to live happily ever after, the thing was monstrously absurd. The general public is not wholly blind to these things. No audience educated up to the point of enjoying "Hamlet" or "Othello" at all would be satisfied with a sugar-candy conclusion to these. The public does ask, however, and asks justly, that there shall be no meaningless agony; and if it prefers tales which inevitably come to a cheerful last chapter, this taste is in the line with the great principle that it is the function of art to uplift and inspire.

It has already been said over and over that it is the office of literature to show the meaning of life, and the meaning of life is not only what it is but what it may be. To paint the actualities of life is only to state a problem, and it is the mission of art to offer a solution. The novel which can go no further than the presentation of the apparent fact is from the higher standpoint futile because it fails to indicate the meaning of that fact; it falls short as art in so far as it fails to justify existence.

Lowell complains: —

> Modern imaginative literature has become so self-conscious, and therefore so melancholy, that Art, which should be "the world's sweet inn," whither we repair for refreshment and repose, has become rather a watering-place, where one's private touch of liver-complaint is exasperated by the affluence of other sufferers whose talk is a narrative of morbid symptoms.
> — *Chaucer.*

We have introduced into fiction that popular and delusive fallacy of emotional socialism which insists not so much that all shall share the best of life, as that none shall escape its worst. The claim that all shall be acquainted with every phase of life is enforced not by an endeavor to make each reader a sharer in the joys and blessings of existence, but by a determined thrusting forward of the pains and shames of humanity. Modern literature has too generally made the profession of treating all facts of life impartially a mere excuse for dealing exclusively with whatever is ugly and degraded, and for dragging to light whatever has been concealed. This is at best as if one used rare cups of Venetian glass for the measuring out of commercial kerosene and vinegar, or precious Grecian urns for the gathering up of the refuse of the streets.

The wise student of literature will never lose sight of the fact that fiction which has not in it an inspiration is to be looked upon as ineffectual, if it is not to be avoided as morbid and unwholesome. Fiction may be sad, it may deal with the darker side of existence; but it should leave the reader with the uplift which comes from the perception that there is in humanity the power to rise by elevation of spirit above the bitterest blight, to triumph over the most cruel circumstances which can befall.

One word must be added in conclusion, and that is the warning that fiction can never take the place of actual life. There is danger in all art that it may win men from interest in real existence. Literature is after all but the interpreter of life, and living is more than all imaginative experience. We need both the book and the deed to round out a full and rich being. It is possible to abuse literature as it is possible to abuse any other gift of the gods. It is not impossible to stultify and benumb the mind by too much novel-reading; but of this there is no need. Fiction properly used and enjoyed is one of the greatest blessings of civilization; and how poor and thin and meagre would life be without it!

XVI

POETRY

THE lover of literature must approach any discussion of poetry with feelings of mingled delight and dread. The subject is one which can hardly fail to excite him to enthusiasm, but it is one with which it is difficult to deal without a declaration of sentiments so strong that they are not likely to be spoken; and it is one, too, upon which so much has been said crudely and carelessly, or wisely and warmly, that any writer must hesitate to add anything to the abundance of words already spoken.

For there have been few things so voluminously discussed as poetry. It is a theme so high that sages could not leave it unpraised; while there is never a penny-a-liner so poor or so mean that he hesitates to write his essay upon the sublime and beautiful art. It is one of the consequences of human vanity that the more subtile and difficult a matter, the more feeble minds feel called upon to cover it with the dust of their empty phrases. The most crowded places are those where angels fear to tread; and it is with reverence not unmixed with fear that any true admirer ventures to speak even his love for the noble art of poetry. No discussion of the study of literature, however, can leave out of the account that which is literature's crown and glory; and of the much that might be said and must be felt, an effort must be made here to set something down.

There are few characteristics more general in the race of man than that responsiveness to rhythm which is the foundation of the love of verse. The sense of symmetry exists in the rudest savage that tattoos the two sides of his face in the same pattern, or strings his necklace of shells in alternating colors. The same feeling is shown by the unæsthetic country matron, the mantel of whose sacredly dark and cold best room is not to her eye properly adorned unless the ugly vase at one end is balanced by another exactly similar ugly vase upon the other. In sound the instinct is yet more strongly marked. The barbaric drum-beat which tells in the quivering sunlight of an African noon that the cannibalistic feast is preparing appeals crudely to the same quality of the human mind which in its refinement responds to the swelling cadences of Mendelssohn's Wedding March or the majestic measures of the Ninth Symphony. The rhythm of the voice in symmetrically arranged words is equally potent in its ability to give pleasure. Savage tribes make the beginnings of literature in inchoate verse. Indeed, so strongly does poetry appeal to men even in the earlier states of civilization that Macaulay seems to have conceived the idea that poetry belongs to an immature stage of growth, — a deduction not unlike supposing the sun to be of no consequence to civilization because it has been worshiped by savages. In the earlier phases of human development, whether of the individual or of the race, the universal instincts are more apparent; and the hold which song takes upon half-barbaric man is simply a proof of how primal and universal is the taste to which it appeals. The sense and enjoyment of rhythm show themselves in a hundred ways in the life and pleasures of primitive races, the vigorous shoots from which is to spring a splendid growth.

Not to go so far back as the dawn of civilization, however, it is sufficient here to recall our own days in the nursery, when Mother Goose, the only universal Alma Mater, with rhymes foolish but rhythmical, meaningless but musical, delighted ears yet too untrained to distinguish sense from folly, but not too young to enjoy the delight of the beating of the voice in metrically arranged accents.

This pleasure in rhythm is persistent, and it is strongly marked even in untrained minds. In natures unspoiled and healthy, natures not bewildered and sophisticated by a false idea of cultivation, or deceived into unsound notions of the real value of poetry, the taste remains sound and good. In the youth of a race this natural enjoyment of verse is gratified by folk-songs. These early forms are naturally undeveloped and simple, but the lays are genuine and wholesome; they possess lasting quality. Different peoples have in differing degrees the power of appreciating verse, but I do not know that any race has. been found to lack it entirely. There is abundant evidence that the Anglo-Saxon and Norman ancestors from whom sprang the English-speaking peoples were in this respect richly endowed, and that they early went far in the development of this power. The old ballads of our language are so rich and so enduringly beautiful that we are proved to come from a stock endowed with a rich susceptibility to poetry. If this taste has not been generally developed it is from some reason other than racial incapacity. Nothing need be looked for in early literatures sweeter and sounder than the fine old ballads of "Chevy Chace," "Tamlane," "Sir Patrick Spens," or "Clerk Saunders." Many a later poet of no mean reputation has failed to strike so deep and true a note as rings through these songs made by forgotten minstrels for a ballad-loving people. There are not too many English-speaking poets to-day who could match the cry of the wraith of Clerk Saunders at the window of his love: —

> Oh, cocks are crowing a merry midnight,
> The wild fowls are boding day;
> Give me my faith and troth again,
> Let me fare on my way. . . .
>
> Cauld mould it is my covering now,
> But and my winding sheet;
> The dew it falls nae sooner down
> Than my resting-place is weet!

How far popular taste has departed from an appreciation of verse that is simple and genuine is shown by those favorite rhymes which are unwearyingly yearned for in the columns of Notes and

Queries, and which reappear with periodic persistence in Answers to Correspondents. In educated persons, it is true, there is still a love of what is really good in verse, but it is far too rare. The general ear and the general taste have become vitiated. There is a melancholy and an amazing number of readers who are pleased only with rhymes of the sort of Will Carleton's "Farm Ballads," the sentimentally inane jingles published in the feminine domestic periodicals, and the rest of what might be called, were not the phrase perilously near to the vulgar, the chewing-gum school of verse.

One of the most serious defects in modern systems of education seems to me to be, as has been said in an earlier talk, an insufficient provision for the development of the imagination. This is nowhere more marked than in the failure to recognize the place and importance of poetry in the training of the mind of youth. It might be supposed that an age which prides itself upon being scientific in its methods would be clever enough to perceive that from the early stages of civilization may well be taken hints for the development of the intellect of the young. Primitive peoples have invariably nourished their growing intelligence and enlarged their imagination by fairy-lore and poetry. The childhood of the individual is in its essentials not widely dissimilar from the childhood of the race; and what was the instinctive and wholesome food for one is good for the other. If our common schools could but omit a good deal of the instruction which is falsely called "practical," because it deals with material issues, and devote the time thus gained to training children to enjoy poetry and to use their imagination, the results would be incalculably better.[1]

The strain and stress of modern life are opposed to the appreciation of any art; and in the case of poetry this difficulty has been increased by a widespread feeling that poetry is after all of little real consequence. It has been held to be an excrescence upon life rather than an essential part of it. It is the tendency of the time to seek for tangible and present results; and men have too generally ceased to appreciate the fact that much which is best is to be reached more surely indirectly than directly. Since of the effects which spring from poetry those most of worth are its remote and intangible results, careless and superficial thinkers have come to look upon song as an unmanly affectation, a thing artificial if not effeminate. This is one of the most absolute and vicious of all intellectual errors. In high and noble truth, poetry is as natural as air; poetry is as virile as war!

It is not easy to discover whence arose the popu-

[1] I say to enjoy poetry. There is much well-meant instruction which is unconsciously conducive to nothing but its detestation. Students who by nature have a fondness for verse are laboriously trained by conscientiously mistaken instructors to regard anything in poetical form as a bore and a torment. The business of a teacher in a preparatory school should be to incite the pupil to love poetry. It is better to make a boy thrill and kindle over a single line than it is to get into his head all the comments made on literature from the beginning of time.

lar feeling of the insignificance of poetry. It is allied to the materialistic undervaluing of all art, and it is probably not unconnected with the ascetic idea that whatever ministers to earthly delight is a hindrance to progress toward the unseen life of another world. Something is to be attributed, no doubt, to the contempt bred by worthless imitations with which facile poetasters have afflicted a long-suffering world; but most of all is the want of an appreciation of the value of poetry to be attributed to the fact that men engrossed in literal and material concerns have not been able to appreciate remote consequences, or to comprehend the utterances of the masters who speak the language of the imagination.

While the world in general, however, has been increasingly unsympathetic toward poetry, the sages have universally concurred in giving to it the highest place in the list of literary achievements. "Poetry," Emerson said, "is the only verity." The same thought is expanded in a passage from Mrs. Browning, in which she speaks of poets as

> — the only truth-tellers now left to God, —
> The only speakers of essential truth,
> Opposed to relative, comparative,
> And temporal truths; the only holders by
> His sun-skirts, through conventual gray glooms;
> The only teachers who instruct mankind
> From just a shadow on a charnel wall
> To find man's veritable stature out,
> Erect, sublime, — the measure of a man.
> —*Aurora Leigh.*

So Wordsworth: —

Poetry is the breath and finer spirit of all knowledge, it is the impassioned expression which is on the face of all science.

It is needless, however, to multiply quotations. The world has never doubted the high respect which those who appreciate poetry have for the art.

It is true also that however general at any time may have been the seeming or real neglect of poetry, the race has not failed to preserve its great poems. The prose of the past, no matter how great its wisdom, has never been able to take with succeeding generations the rank held by the masterpieces of the poets. Mankind has seemed not unlike one who affects to hold his jewels in little esteem, it may be, yet like the jewel owner it has guarded them with constant jealousy. The honor-roll of literature is the world's list of great poets. The student of literature is not long in discovering that his concern is far more largely with verse than with anything else that the wit of mankind has devised to write. However present neglect may at any time appear to show the contrary, the long-abiding regard of the race declares beyond peradventure that it counts poetry as most precious among all its intellectual treasures.

XVII

THE TEXTURE OF POETRY

In discussing poetry it is once more necessary to begin with something which will serve us as a definition. No man can imprison the essence of an art in words; and it is not to be understood that a formal definition can be framed which shall express all that poetry is and means. Its more obvious characteristics, however, may be phrased, and even an incomplete formula is often useful. There have been almost as many definitions of poetry made already as there have been writers on literature, some of them intelligible and some of them open to the charge of incomprehensibility. Schopenhauer, for instance, defined poetry as the art of exciting by words the power of the imagination; a phrase so broad that it is easily made to cover all genuine literature. It will perhaps be sufficient for our purpose here if we say that poetry is the embodiment in metrical, imaginative language of passionate emotion.

By metrical language is meant that which is systematically rhythmical. Much prose is rhythmical. Indeed it is difficult to conceive of fine or delicate prose which has not rhythm to some degree, and oratorical prose is usually distinguished by this. The Bible abounds in excellent examples; as, for instance, this passage from Job: —

> Hell is naked before Him, and destruction hath no covering; He stretcheth out the north over the empty place, and hangeth the earth upon nothing. He bindeth up the waters in his thick clouds; and the cloud is not rent under them. He holdeth back the face of His throne, and spreadeth His cloud upon it. He hath compassed the waters with bounds until the day and night come to an end. The pillars of heaven tremble, and are astonished at His reproof. He divideth the sea with His power, and by His understanding He smiteth through the proud. — *Job*, xxvi. 6–12.

Here, as in all fine prose, there is a rhythm which is marked, and at times almost regular; but it is not ordered by a system, as it must be in the simplest verse of poetry. Take, by way of contrast, a stanza from the superb chorus to Artemis in "Atalanta in Calydon:" —

> Come with bows bent and with emptying of quivers,
>   Maiden most perfect, lady of light,
> With a noise of winds and many rivers,
>   With a clamor of waters and with might;
> Bind on thy sandals, O thou most fleet,
> Over the splendor and speed of thy feet;
> For the faint east quickens, the wan west shivers,
> Round the feet of the day and the feet of the night.

Here the rhythm is systematized according to regular laws, and so becomes metrical. The effect upon the ear in prose is largely due to rhythm, but metrical effects are entirely within the province of poetry.

This difference between rhythmical and metrical language would seem to be sufficiently obvious, but the difficulty which many students have in appreciating it may make it worth while to give another illustration. The following passage from Edmund Burke, that great master of sonorous English, is strongly and finely rhythmical: —

> Because we are so made as to be affected at such spectacles with melancholy sentiments upon the unstable condition of mortal prosperity, and the tremendous uncertainty of human greatness; because in those natural feelings we learn great lessons; because in events like these our passions instruct our reason; because when kings are hurled from their thrones by the Supreme Director of this great drama, and become objects of insult to the base, and of pity to the good, we behold such disasters in the moral, as we should behold a miracle in the physical order of things. — *Reflections on the Revolution in France.*

So markedly rhythmical is this, indeed, that it would take but little to change it into metre: —

> Because we are so made as to be moved by spectacles like these with melancholy sentiments of the unstable case of mortal things, and the uncertainty of human greatness here; because in those our natural feelings we may learn great lessons too; because in such events our passions teach our reason well; because when kings are hurled down from their thrones, etc.

There is no longer any dignity in this. It has become a sort of sing-song, neither prose nor yet poetry. The sentiments are not unlike those of a familiar passage in Shakespeare : —

> This is the state of man; to-day he puts forth
> The tender leaves of hopes; to-morrow blossoms,

And bears his blushing honors thick upon him :
The third day comes a frost, a killing frost ;
And, — when he thinks, good easy man, full surely
His greatness is a ripening, — nips his root,
And then he falls, as I do.

Henry VIII., iii. 2.

In the extract from Burke a sense of weakness and even of flatness is produced by the rearrangement of the accents so that they are made regular ; while in the verse of Shakespeare the sensitive ear is very likely troubled by the single misplaced accent in the first line. In any mood save the poetic metre seems an artificiality and an affectation, but in that mood it is as natural and as necessary as air to the lungs.

Besides being metrical the language of poetry must be imaginative. By imaginative language is meant that which not only conveys imaginative conceptions, but which is itself full of force and suggestion; language which not only expresses ideas and emotions, but which by its own power evokes them. Imaginative language is marked by the most vivid perception on the part of the writer of the connotive effect of words; it conveys even more by implication than by direct denotation. It may of course be used in poetry or prose. In the passage from Job just quoted, the use of such phrases as "empty place," "hangeth the earth upon nothing," convey more by what they suggest to the mind than by their literal assertion. The writer has evidently used them with a vital and vivid understanding of their suggestiveness. He realizes to the full their office to convey impressions so subtle that they cannot be given by direct and literal diction.

Poetry is made up of words and phrases which glow with this richness of intention. When Shakespeare speaks of skin "smooth as monumental alabaster," how much is added to the idea by the epithet "monumental," the suggestion of the polished and protected stone, enshrined on a tomb; how much is due to association and implication in such phrases as the "reverberate hills," "parting is such sweet sorrow," "the white wonder of dear Juliet's hand," "and sleep in dull, cold marble," — phrases all of which have a literal significance plain enough, yet of which this literal meaning is of small account beside that which they evoke. Poetic diction naturally and inevitably melts into figures, as when we read of "the shade of melancholy boughs," "the spendthrift sun," "the bubble reputation," "the inaudible and noiseless foot of time;" but the point here is that even in its literal words there is constantly the sense and the employment of implied meanings. It is by no means necessarily figures to which language owes the quality of being imaginative. Broadly speaking, a style may be said to be imaginative in proportion as the writer has realized and intended its suggestions.

The language of prose is often imaginative to a high degree, but seldom if ever to that extent or with that deliberate purpose which in verse is nothing less than essential. Genuine poetry differs from prose in the entire texture of its web. From the same threads the loom may weave plain stuff or richest brocade; and thus of much the same words are made prose and poetry. The difference lies chiefly in the fashion of working.

The essentials of the manner of poetry being language metrical and imaginative, the essential of the matter is that it be the expression of passionate emotion. By passionate emotion is meant any feeling, powerful or delicate, which is capable of filling the whole soul; of taking possession for the time being of the entire man. It may be fierce hate, enthralling love, ambition, lust, rage, jealousy, joy, sorrow, any over-mastering mood, or it may be one of those intangible inclinations, those moods of mist, ethereal as hazes in October, those caprices of pleasure or sadness which Tennyson had the art so marvelously to reproduce. Passionate emotion is by no means necessarily intense, but it is engrossing. For the time being, at least, it seems to absorb the whole inner consciousness.

It is the completeness with which such a mood takes possession of the mind, so that for the moment it is to all intents and purposes the man himself, that gives it so great an importance in human life and makes it the fitting and the sole essential theme of the highest art. Behind all serious human effort lies the instinctive sense of the fitness of things. The artist must always convince that his end is worthy of the means which he employs to reach it; and it follows naturally that the writer who uses imaginative diction and the elaborateness of metre must justify this by what he embodies in them. Metrical forms are as much out of place in treating of the material concerns of life as would be court robes or religious rites in the reaping of a field or the selling of a cargo of wool. The poet is justified in his use of all the resources of form and of poetic diction by the fact that the message which he is endeavoring to convey is high and noble; that the meaning which he attempts to impart is so profoundly subtle as to be inexpressible unless the words which he employs are assisted by the language of rhythm and metre.

That the reader unconsciously recognizes the fact that the essential difference in the office of prose and poetry makes inevitable a difference also of method, is shown by his dissatisfaction when the writer of prose invades the province of poetry. The arrangement of the words of prose into systematic rhythm produces at once an effect of weakness and of insincerity. Dickens in some of his attempts to reach deep pathos has made his prose metrical with results most disastrous. The mood of poetry is so elevated that metrical conventions seem appropriate and natural; whereas in the mood of even the most emotional prose they appear fantastical and affected. The difference is not unlike that between the speaking and the singing voice. A man who sang in conversation, or even in a highly excited oration, would simply make himself ridiculous. In song this manner of using the voice is not only natural but inevitable and delightful. What would be uncalled for in the most exalted moods of the prose writer is natural and fitting in the case of the poet, because the poet is endeavoring to embody, in language the most deep, the most high, the most delicate experiences of which humanity is capable. The form is with him a part of his normal language. To say in prose : " My love is like a red rose newly sprung in June, or like a melody beautifully played," means not much. Yet the words themselves are not widely varied from those in which Burns conveys the same ideas with so great an added beauty, and so much more emotional force : —

> Oh, my luve 's like a red, red rose
> That 's newly sprung in June;
> Oh, my luve 's like a melodie
> That 's sweetly played in tune.

The metrical cadences woo the ear like those of a melody sweetly played, and to that which the words may say or suggest they add an effect yet more potent and delightful.

A moment's consideration of these facts enables one to estimate rightly the stricture made by Plato : —

You have often seen what a poor appearance the tales of poets make when stripped of the colors which music puts upon them, and recited in prose. They are like faces which were never really beautiful, but only blooming, and now the bloom of youth has passed away from them.

It would be more just and more exact to say that they are like the framework of a palace from which have been stripped the slabs of precious marble which covered it. It is neither more nor less reasonable to object to poetry that its theme told in prose is slight or dull than it would be to scorn St. Peter's because its rafters and ridgepole might not be attractive if they stood out bare against the sky. The form is in poetry as much an integral part as walls and roof and dome, statues and jewel-like marbles, are part of the temple.

Leaving out of consideration those peculiarities such as rhyme and special diction, which although often of much effect are not essential since poetry may be great without them, it is sufficiently exact for a general examination to say that the effects of poetry are produced by the threefold union of ideas, suggestion, and melody. In the use of ideas poetry is on much the same footing as prose, except in so far as it deals with exalted moods which have no connection with thoughts which are mean or commonplace. In the use of suggestion poetry but carries farther the means employed in imaginative prose. Melody may be said practically to be its own prerogative. The smoothest flow of rhythmical prose falls far below the melodious cadences of metrical language; and in this manner of appeal to the senses and the soul of man verse has no rival save music itself.

These three qualities may be examined separately. Verse may be found in which there is almost nothing but melody, divorced from suggestion or ideas. There are good examples in Edward Lear's "Nonsense Songs," in which there is an intentional lack of sense; or in the "Alice" books, as, for instance: —

> And as in uffish thought he stood,
> The Jabberwock, with eyes of flame,
> Came whiffling through the tulgy wood,
> And burbled as it came! . . .
>
> "And hast thou slain the Jabberwock?
> Come to my arms, my beamish boy!
> O frabjous day! Callooh! Callay!"
> He chortled in his joy.

Or one may take something which will convey no idea and no suggestion beyond that which comes with sound and rhythm. Here is a verse once made in sport to pass as a folk-song in an unknown tongue: —

> Apaulthee kong lay laylarthay;
> Ameeta tinta prown,
> Lay lista, lay larba, lay moona long,
> Toolay échola doundoolay koko elph zong,
> Im lay melplartha bountaina brown.

This is a collection of unmeaning syllables, and yet to the ear it is a pleasure. The examples may seem trivial, but they serve to illustrate the fact that there is magic in the mere sound of words, meaning though they have none.

The possibility of pleasing solely by the arrangement and choice of words in verse has been a snare to more than one poet; as a neglect of melody has been the fault of others. In much of the later work of Swinburne it is evident that the poet became intoxicated with the mere beauty of sound, and forgot that poetry demands thought as well as melody; while the reader is reluctantly forced to acknowledge that in some of the verse of Browning there is a failure to recognize that melody is an element as essential as thought.

As verse may be found which has little but melody, so is it possible to find verse in which there is practically nothing save melody and suggestion. In "Ulalume" Poe has given an instance of the effect possible from the combining of these with but the thinnest thread of idea: —

> The skies they were ashen and sober;
> The leaves they were crispèd and sere, —
> The leaves they were withering and sere;
> It was night in the lonesome October,
> Of my most immemorial year;
> It was hard by the dim lake of Auber,
> In the misty mid-region of Weir —
> It was down by the dark tarn of Auber,
> In the ghoul-haunted woodland of Weir.

There is here no definite train of thought. It is an attempt to convey a certain mood by combining mysterious and weird suggestion with melody enticing and sweet.

A finer example is the closing passage in "Kubla Khan." The suggestions are more vivid, and the imagination far more powerful.

> A damsel with a dulcimer
> In a vision once I saw;
> It was an Abyssinian maid,
> And on her dulcimer she played,
> Singing of Mount Abora.
> Could I revive within me
> Her symphony and song,
> To such deep delight 't would win me,
> That with music loud and long,
> I would build that dome in air,
> That sunny dome; those caves of ice;
> And all who heard should see them there,
> And all should cry: "Beware! Beware!
> His flashing eyes, his floating hair;

> Weave a circle round him thrice,
> And close your eyes with holy dread,
> For he on honey-dew hath fed,
> And drunk the milk of Paradise."

Here there is a more evident succession of ideas than in "Ulalume;" but in both the effect is almost entirely produced by the music and the suggestion, with very little aid from ideas.

How essential to poetry are melody and suggestion is at once evident when one examines verse which contains ideas without these fundamental qualities. Wordsworth, great as he is at his best, affords ready examples here. The following is by no means the least poetical passage in "The Prelude," but it is sufficiently far from being poetry in any high sense to serve as an illustration:—

> I was a better judge of thoughts than words,
> Misled in estimating words, not only
> By common inexperience of youth,
> But by the trade of classic niceties,
> The dangerous craft of culling term and phrase
> From languages that want the living voice
> To carry meaning to the natural heart.

Here are ideas, but there is no emotion, and the thing could be said better in prose. It is as fatal to try to express in poetry what is not elevated enough for poetic treatment as it is to endeavor to say in prose those high things which can be embodied by poetry only. Melody alone, or suggestiveness alone, is better than ideas alone if there is to be an attempt to produce the effect of poetry.

Poetry which is complete and adequate adds

melody and suggestion to that framework of ideas which is to them as the skeleton to flesh and blood. Any of the great lyrics of the language might be given as examples. The reader has but to open his Shakespeare's "Sonnets" at random, as for instance, at this: —

> From you have I been absent in the spring,
> When proud-pied April, dressed in all his trim,
> Hath put a spirit of youth in every thing,
> That heavy Saturn laugh'd and leap'd with him.
> Yet nor the lays of birds, nor the sweet smell
> Of different flowers in odor and in hue,
> Could make me any summer's story tell,
> Or from their proud lap pluck them where they grew:
> Nor did I wonder at the lily's white,
> Nor praise the deep vermilion in the rose;
> They were but sweet, but figures of delight,
> Drawn after you, you pattern of all those.
> Yet seem'd it winter still, and, you away,
> As with your shadow I with these did play.

It is not necessary to carry this analysis farther. The object of undertaking it is to impress upon the reader the fact that in poetry form is an essential element in the language of the art. The student must realize that the poet means his rhythm as truly as and in the same measure that he means the thought; and that to attempt to appreciate poetry without sensitiveness to melody is as hopeless as would be a similar attempt to try to appreciate music. When Wordsworth said that poetry is inevitable, he meant the metre no less than the thought; he wished to convey the fact that the impassioned mood breaks into melody of word as the full heart breaks into song. The true poem is the embodiment of what can be expressed in no other way than by that especial combination of idea, suggestion, and sound. The thought, the hint, and the music are united in one unique and individual whole.

XVIII

POETRY AND LIFE

VITALLY to appreciate what poetry is, it is necessary to realize what are its relations to life. Looked at in itself its essentials are emotion which is capable of taking entire possession of the consciousness, and the embodiment of this emotion by the combined effects of imaginative language and melodious form. It is still needful, however, to consider how this art acts upon human beings, and why there has been claimed for it so proud a preeminence among the arts.

Why, for instance, should Emerson speak of the embodiment of mere emotion as "the only verity," Wordsworth as "the breath and finer spirit of all knowledge," and why does Mrs. Browning call poets "the only truth-tellers"? The answer briefly is: Because consciousness is identical with emotion, and consciousness is life. For all practical purposes man exists but in that he feels. The universe concerns him in so far as it touches his feelings, and it concerns him no farther. That is for man most essential which comes most near to the conditions of his existence. Pure and ideal emotion is essential truth in the sense that it approaches most nearly to the consciousness, — that is, to the actual being of the race.

I am aware that this sounds dangerously like an attempt to be darkly metaphysical; but it is impossible to talk on high themes without to some extent using high terms. It is useless to hope to put into words all the mysteries of the relations of art to life, yet it is not impossible to approximate somewhat to what must be the truth of the matter, although in doing it one inevitably runs the risk of seeming to attempt to say what cannot be said. What I have been endeavoring to convey will perhaps be plainer if I say that for purposes of our discussion man is practically alive only in so far as he realizes life. This realization of life, this supreme triumph of inner consciousness, comes to him through his feelings, — indeed, is perhaps to be considered as identical with his feelings. His sensations affect him only by the emotions which they excite. His emotion, in a word, is the measure of his existence. Now the emotion of man always responds, in a degree marked by appreciation, to certain presentations of the relation of things, to certain considerations of the nature of human life, and above all to certain demonstrations of the possibilities of human existence. If these are made actual and clear to the mind, they cannot fail to arouse that engrossing realization which is the height of consciousness. To enable a man to seize with his imagination the ideal of love or hate, of fear or courage, of shame or honor, is to make him kindle and thrill. It is to make him for the time being thoroughly and richly alive, and it is to increase greatly his power of essential life.

These are the things which most deeply touch human creatures; they are the universal in that they appeal to all sane hearts and minds; they are the eternal as measured by mortal existence because they have power to touch the men of all time; hence they are the real truths; they are, for beings under the conditions of earthly existence, the only verities.

The ordinary life of man is not unlike the feeble flame of a miner's lamp, half smothered in some underground gallery until a draught of vital air kindles it into sudden glow and sparkle. Most human beings have but a dull flicker of half-alive consciousness until some outward breath causes it to flash into quick and quivering splendor. Poetry is that divine air, that breeze from unscaled heights of being, the kindling breath by which the spark becomes a flame.

It is but as a means of conveying the essential truth which is the message of poetry, that the poet employs obvious truth. The facts which impress themselves upon the outer senses are to him merely a language by means of which he seeks to impart the higher facts that are apprehended only by the inner self; those facts of emotion which it is his office as a seer to divine and to interpret. The swineherd and the wandering minstrel saw the same wood and sky and lake; but to one they were earth and air and water; while to the other they were the outward and visible embodiment of the spirit of beauty which is eternal though earth and sea and sky vanish. To Peter Bell the primrose by the river's brim was but a primrose and nothing more; to the poet it was the symbol and the embodiment of loveliness, the sign of an eternal truth. To the laborer going afield in the early light the dewdrops are but so much water, wetting unpleasantly his shoes; to Browning it was a symbol of the embodiment in woman of all that is pure and holy when he sang: —

There 's a woman like a dew-drop, she 's so purer than the purest.

It is evident from what has been said that in reading poetry it is necessary to penetrate through the letter to the spirit. I have already spoken at length in a former lecture upon the need of knowing the language of literature, and of being in sympathy with the mood of the writer. This is especially true in regard to poetry, since poetry becomes great in proportion as it deals with the spirit rather than with the letter. "We are all poets when we read a poem well," Carlyle has said. It is only by entering into the mood and by sharing the exaltation of the poet that we are able to appreciate his message. A poem is like a window of stained glass. From without one may be able to gain some general idea of its design and to guess crudely at its hues; but really to perceive its beauty, its richness of design, its sumptuousness of color, one must stand within the very sanctuary itself.

It is partly from the lack of sensitiveness of the imagination of the reading public, I believe, that in the latter half of this century the novel has grown into a prominence so marked. The great mass of readers no longer respond readily to poetry, and fiction is in a sense a simplification of the language of imagination so that it may be comprehended by those who cannot rise to the heights of verse. In this sense novels might almost be called the kindergarten of the imagination. In fiction, emotional experiences are translated into the language of ordinary intellectual life; whereas in poetry they are phrased in terms of the imagination, pure and simple. There can be no question of the superiority of the means employed by the poet. Much which is embodied in verse cannot be expressed by prose of any sort, no matter how exalted that prose may be; but for the ordinary intelligence the language of prose is far more easily comprehensible.

What I have been saying, however, may seem to be so general and theoretical that I may be held not yet fairly to have faced that issue at which I hinted in the beginning, the issue which Philistine minds raise bluntly: What is the use of poetry? Philistines are willing to concede that there is a sensuous pleasure to be gained from verse. They are able to perceive how those who care for such things may find an enervating enjoyment in the linked sweetness of cadence melting into cadence, in musical line and honeyed phrase. What they are utterly unable to understand is how thoughtful men, men alive to the practical needs and the real interests of the race, can speak of poetry as if it were a thing of genuine importance in the history and development of mankind. It would not be worth while to attempt an answer to this for the benefit of the Philistines. They are a folk who are so completely ignorant of the higher good of life that it is impossible to make them understand. Their conception of value does not reach beyond pecuniary and physical standards; they comprehend nothing which is not expressed in material terms. One who attempted to describe a symphony to a deaf man would not be more at a loss for terms than must be he who attempts to set forth the worth of art to those ignorant of real values. The question may be answered, but to those who most need to be instructed in regard to æsthetic values any answer must forever remain unintelligible.

There are, however, many sincere and earnest seekers after truth who are unable to clear up their ideas when they come in contact, as they must every day, with the assumption that poetry is but the plaything of idle men and women, a thing not only unessential but even frivolous. For them it is worth while to formulate some sort of a statement; although to do this is like making the attempt to declare why the fragrance of the rose is sweet or why the hue of its petals gives delight.

In the first place, then, the use of poetry is to nourish the imagination. I have spoken earlier of the impossibility of fulfilling the higher functions of life without this faculty. A common error regards imagination as a quality which has to do with rare and exceptional experiences; as a power of inventing whimsical and impossible thoughts; as a sort of jester to beguile idle moments of the mind. In reality imagination is to the mental being what blood is to the physical man. Upon it the intellect and the emotional consciousness alike depend for nourishment. Without it the mind is powerless to seize or to make really its own anything which lies outside of actual experience. Without it the broker could not so fully realize his cunning schemes as to manipulate the market and control the price of stocks; without it the inventor could devise no new machine, the scientist grasp no fresh secret of laws which govern the universe. It is the divine power in virtue of which man subdues the world to his uses. In a word, imagination is that faculty which distinguishes man from brute.

It is the beginning of wisdom to know; it is the culmination of wisdom to feel. The intellect accumulates; the emotion assimilates. What we learn, we possess; but what we feel, we are. The perception acquires, and the imagination realizes; and thus it is that only through the imagination can man build up and nourish that inner being which is the true and vital self. To cultivate the imagination, therefore, is an essential — nay, more; it is the one essential means of insuring the progression of the race. This is the great office of all art, but perhaps most obviously is it the noble prerogative and province of poetry. "In the imagination," wrote Coleridge, "is the distinguishing characteristic of man as a progressive being." To kindle into flame the dull embers of this god-like attribute is the first office of poetry; and were this all, it would lift the art forever above every cumbering material care and engrossing intellectual interest.

In the second place, the use of poetry is to give man knowledge of his unrecognized experiences or his unrealized capacities of feeling. The poet speaks what many have felt, but what none save he can say. He accomplishes the hitherto impossible. He makes tangible and subject the vague emotions which disquiet us as if they were elusive ghosts haunting the dwelling of the soul, unsubdued and oppressive in their mystery. The joy of a moment he has fixed for all time; the throb gone almost before it is felt he has made captive; to the evasive emotion he has given immortality. In a word, it is his office to confer upon men dominion over themselves.

Third, it is poetry which nourishes and preserves the optimism of the race. Poetry is essentially optimistic. It raises and encourages by fixing the mind upon the possibilities of life. Even when it bewails what is gone, when it weeps lost perfection, vanished joy, and crushed love, the reader receives from the poetic form, from the uplift of metrical inspiration, a sense that the possibilities of existence overwhelm individual pain. The fact that such blessings could and may exist is not only consolation when fate has wrenched them away, but the vividness with which they are recalled may almost make them seem to be relived. That

> A sorrow's crown of sorrow is remembering happier things,

is not the whole story. In times of deepest woe it is this very remembrance which makes it possible to live on at all. The unconscious and the inevitable lesson of all true art, moreover, is that the possibility of beauty in life is compensation for the anguish which its existence entails. The poet who weeps for the lost may have no word of comfort to offer, but the fact that life itself is of supreme possibilities is shown inevitably and persuasively by the fact that he is so deeply moved. He could not be thus stricken had he not known very ecstasies of joy; and his message to the race is that such bliss has been and thus may be again. More than this, the fact that he in his anguish instinctively turns to art is the most eloquent proof that however great may be the sorrows of life there is for them an alleviating balm in æsthetic enjoyment. He may speak of

> Beauty that must die,
> And Joy whose hand is ever at his lips,
> Bidding adieu;

but with the very thought of the brevity is coupled an exquisite sense of both beauty and joy in ever fresh renewal, so that the reader knows a subtle thrill of pleasure even at the mention of pain. Poe's proposition that poetry should be restricted to sorrowful themes probably arose from a more or less conscious feeling that the expression of despair is the surest means of conveying vividly a sense of the value of what is gone; and whether Poe went so far as to realize it or not the fact is that the passion of loss most surely expresses the possible bliss of possession. Even when it would, art cannot deny the worth and the glory of existence. The word of denial is chanted to a strain which inspires and affirms. Even when he would be most pessimistic the genuine poet must perforce preach in deathless tones the gospel of optimism.

Fourth, poetry is the original utterance of the ideas of the world. It is easy and not uncommon to regard the art of the poet as having little to do with the practical conduct of life; yet there is no man in civilization who does not hold opinions and theories, thoughts and beliefs, which he owes to the poets. Thought is not devised in the marketplace. What thinkers have divined in secret is there shown openly by its results. Every poet of genius remakes the world. He leaves the stamp of his imagination upon the whole race, and philosophers reason, scientists explore, money-changers scheme, tradesmen haggle, and farmers plough or sow, all under conditions modified by what has been divulged in song. The poet is the great thinker, whose thought, translated, scattered, diluted, spilled upon the ground and gathered up again, is the inspiration and the guide of mankind.

If this seem extravagant, think for a little. Reflect in what civilization differs from savagery; consider not the accidental and outward circumstance, but the fundamental causes upon which these depend. If you endeavor to find adequately expressed the ideals of honor, of truth, of love, and of aspiration which are behind all the development of mankind, it is to the poets that you turn instinctively. It is possible to go farther than this. Knowledge is but a perception of relations. The conception of the universe is too vast to be assimilated all at once, but every perception of the way in which one part is related to another, one fact to another, one thing to the rest, helps toward a realization of the ultimate truth. It is the poet who first discerns and proclaims the relations of those facts which the experience of the race accumulates. From the particular he deduces the general, from the facts he perceives the principles which underlie them. The general, that is, in its relation to that emotional consciousness which is the real life of man; the principles which take hold not upon material things only, but upon the very conditions of human existence. All abstract truth has sprung from poetry as rain comes from the sea. Changed, diffused, carried afar and often altered almost beyond recognition, the thought of the world is but the manifestation of the imagination of the world; and it has found its first tangible expression in poetry.

Fifth, poetry is the instructor in beauty. No small thing is human happiness, and human happiness is nourished on beauty. Poetry opens the eyes of men to loveliness in earth and sky and sea, in flower and weed, in tree and rock and stream, in things common and things afar alike. It is by the interpretation of the poet that mankind in general is aware of natural beauty; and it is hardly less true that the beauty of moral and emotional worlds would be practically unknown were it not for these high interpreters. The race has first become aware of all ethereal and elusive loveliness through the song of the poet, sensitive to see and skillful to tell. For its beauty in and of itself, and for its revelation of the beauty of the universe, both material and intangible, poetry is to the world a boon priceless and peerless.

Sixth, poetry is the creator and preserver of ideals. The ideal is the conception of the existence beyond what is of that which may and should be. It is the measure of the capability of desire. "Man's desires are limited by his perceptions," says William Blake; "none can desire what he has not perceived." What man can receive, what it is possible for him to enjoy, is limited to what he is able to wish for. The ideal is the highest point to which his wish has been able to attain, and upon the advancement of this point must depend the increasing of the possibilities of individual experience. With the growth of ideals, moreover, comes the constant, however slow, realization of them. So true is this that it almost affords a justification of the belief that whatever mankind really desires must in the end be realized from the very fact that it is desired. Be that as it may, an ideal is the perception of a higher reality. It is the recognition of essential as distinguished from accidental truth; the comprehension of the eternal principle which must underlie every fact. It is a realization of the meaning of existence; a piercing through the transient appearance to the fundamental and the enduring. The reader who finds himself caught away like St. Paul to the third heaven — " whether in the body I cannot tell; or whether out of the body I cannot tell " — has no need to ask whether life is merely eating and drinking, getting and spending, marrying and giving in marriage. He has for that transcendent moment lived the real life; he has tasted the possibilities of existence; he has for one glorious instant realized the ideal. When a poem has carried him out of himself and the material present which we call the real, then the verse has been for him as a chariot of fire in which he has been swirled upward to the very heart of the divine.

When not actually under the influence of this high exalting power of poetry most men have a strange reluctance to admit that it is possible for them to be so moved; and thus it may easily happen that what has just been said may seem to the reader extravagant and florid. There are happily few, however, to whom there have not come moments of inner illumination, few who cannot if they will call up times when the imagination has carried them away, and the delight of being so borne above the actual was a revelation and a joy not easily to be put into word. Recalling such an experience, you will not find it difficult to understand what is meant by the claim that poetry creates in the mind of man an ideal which in turn it justifies also.

Lastly and above all, the use of poetry is — poetry.

> 'T is the deep music of the rolling world
> Kindling within the strings of the waved air
> Æolian modulations.

It is vain to endeavor to put into word the worth and office of poetry. At the last we are brought face to face with the fact that anything short of itself is inadequate to do it justice. To read a single page of a great singer is more potent than to pore over volumes in his praise. A single lyric puts to shame the most elaborate analysis or the most glowing eulogy; in the end there is no resource but to appeal to the inner self which is the true man; since in virtue of what is most deep and noble in the soul, each may perceive for himself that poetry is its own supreme justification; that there is no need to discuss the relation of poetry to life, since poetry is the expression of life in its best and highest possibilities.

INDEX

INDEX

Abbot, J. S. C., "Rollo," 201.
Addison, 66.
Advertising, 168-170.
Æschylus, 149.
Aldrich, T. B., "Story of a Bad Boy," 11, 15.
Allusions, Biblical, 98-101; to folk-lore, 106; historical, 103-106; literary, 107-108; mythological, 101-103.
Amiel, "Journal Intime," 7.
Amiot, 90.
Andersen, Hans Christian, 196.
Apprehension, 74.
Ariosto, 143.
Art, conventions in, 89; deals with the typical, 6; end of, 87; good, 22; origin of, 3-5; sanity of, 174; truth in, 206; truth of, 209; vs. science, 32.
Artist, office of, 207.
Asbjörnsen, 196.
Augustine, St., "Confessions," 7.
Austen, Jane, 189.

Ballads, 222.
Balzac, 189.
Barrie, J. M., 211.
Bible, 101, 140, 142, 145, 197; allusions to, 98-101; as a classic, 143-147; books of, characterized, 146; quoted, 100, 228; Revised Version vs. King James, 146.
Black, William, 13, 211.
Blackmore, R. D., 211.
Blake, William, 54, 66; quoted, 58, 121, 252.
Boccaccio, 143.
Breeding, good, 204.
Brontë, Charlotte, 189.
Broughton, Rhoda, 185.
Browning, Mrs. E. B., quoted, 8, 132, 225, 241; "Sonnets from the Portuguese," 7-9.
Browning, Robert, 92, 155, 179, 180; "Childe Roland to the Dark Tower Came," 48; lack of melody, 236; obscure in allusions, 106; "Prospice," 13; quoted, 244; "The Ring and the Book," 180.
Bunyan, John, "Pilgrim's Progress," 129.

Burke, Edmund, quoted, 229.
Burns, quoted, 234.
Byron, Lord, 11, 12; quoted, 104.

Cable, G. W., 211.
Carleton, Will, "Farm Ballads," 223.
Carlyle, Thomas, 42; quoted, 244.
Carroll, Lewis, quoted, 236.
Cervantes, 133, 140, 143; "Don Quixote," 129, 189.
Character, 56.
Chaucer, Geoffrey, 78, 116, 123, 124, 140, 142, 146; as a classic, 151-152; Lowell on, 114; quoted, 114.
Children, education of, 193-196, 223; reading of, 195-198.
Civilization, 204.
Classic, defined, 127.
Classics, 176, 177; cause of the neglect of, 132-134; test of, 130.
"Clerk Saunders," 222.
Coleridge, S. T., 54, 66; "Hymn Before Sunrise," etc., 75; quoted, 145, 237, 247.
Collins, William, 66.
Comprehension, 74.
Conventions, 88-92.
Cowper, William, quoted, 79.
Crawford, F. M., 211.
Critics, use of, 70.

Dante, 58, 78, 140, 142, 146; as a classic, 150-151.
Darwin, Charles, 55.
D'Aulnoy, Countess, 196.
D'Aurevilly, Barbey, 169.
Defoe, 66; "Robinson Crusoe," 197.
De Gasparin, Madame, "The Near and the Heavenly Horizons," 48.
De Maupassant, Guy, 182.
Dekker, Thomas, quoted, 115.
Dickens, Charles, 179, 180, 189; his metrical prose, 233.
Doyle, A. Conan, 211; quoted, 134.
Dryden, John, 66, 146; quoted, 152.
"Duchess," The, 13, 185.
Dumas, A., père, 182, 189; "D'Artagnan Romances," 27, 92.

Edgeworth, Maria, 201.
Education, use of poetry in, 223.
Eliot, George, 180, 187, 189.

Emerson, R. W., 179, 180; on translations, 148; quoted, 43, 47, 103, 225, 241.
Emotion, 241-245; fashion in, 15; genuine, 68; tests of genuineness of, 10-20.
Etiquette, 204.
Euripides, 149.
Experience the test of art, 10.

Fairy stories, 196-197.
Fiction, truth in, 188.
Fielding, Henry, 66.
Folk-lore, 223.
Folk-songs, 137-139, 221-222.
French authors, 170.
Fuller, Margaret, 86.

Genius, 20, 250.
Gibbon, Edward, quoted, 74.
Gladstone, W. E., 168.
Goethe, quoted, 36, 178.
Goldsmith, Oliver, 66.
Gower, John, 116.
Gray, Thomas, quoted, 103.
Greek literature, 149, 150.
Greek sculpture, 150.
Greek tragedians, 143, 148.
Greeks, sanity of the, 148.
Grimm, The Brothers, 194, 196.

Haggard, Rider, "She," 26.
Hannay, James, quoted, 57.
Hardy, Thomas, "Far from the Madding Crowd," 181; "The Return of the Native," 181, 208; "Tess of the D'Urbervilles," 181; "Under the Greenwood Tree," 181.
Harris, J. C., "Uncle Remus," 197.
Hawthorne, Nathaniel, 179, 180, 189; Arthur Dimmesdale, 201; "The Marble Faun," 92; quoted, 83; "The Scarlet Letter," 2, 13, 201, 208, 214; "Tanglewood Tales," 197; "The Wonder-Book," 197.
Hazlitt, William, quoted, 113.
"Helen of Kirconnell," 13, 138.
Homer, 58, 78, 123, 131, 140, 142, 146, 151; as a classic, 147-150.
Hope, Anthony, 211.
Hugo, Victor, 189; "Les Misérables," 92, 208.
Hunt, Leigh, quoted, 84.
Hunt, W. M., quoted, 62.

Ibsen, 172, 173, 177; "The Doll's House," 18; "Ghosts," 173.
Imagination, 93, 246-248, 253; and thought, 251; creative, 111; the realizing faculty, 19; reality of, 54.
Imaginative language, defined, 230-231.
Imaginative quality, test of, 93.
Impressionism, 69.
Interest, temporary and permanent, 127-129.

Irreverence, 87.
Isaiah, 146, 150.

James, Henry, quoted, 203.
Jewett, Sarah O., Miss, 211.
Job, 146, 230.
Johnson, Samuel, quoted, 84.
Jonson, Ben, quoted, 83.
Judd, Sylvester, "Margaret," 30.

Keats, John, 54, 92, 112; letters to Miss Brawne, 62; "Ode to a Grecian Urn," 17; quoted, 94, 102, 249.
Kingsley, Charles, 180.
Kipling, Rudyard, 182; "Jungle Books," 197, 213.

Laboulaye, Édouard, 196.
Lamb, Charles, 133; quoted, 196.
Language, imaginative, defined, 230-231.
Lear, Edward, 235.
Lessing, "Nathan the Wise," 48.
Lincoln, Abraham, "Gettysburg Address," 112.
Literature, books about, 65-68; convincing, 14; defined, 1-32; didactic, 201; early, 136; eighteenth century, 65, 66; gossip about, 62-65; history of, 65; juvenile, 193-195; morbid, 20, 177, 178; office of, 46-59; relative rank, 31; study of, defined, 33-44, 60-68; study of, difficult, 72; talk about, 40-43; a unit, 154; vs. science, 55.
"Littell's Living Age," 39.
Longfellow, H. W., 181.
Lowell, J. R., 67; quoted, 78, 102, 114, 173, 216.

Macaulay, T. B., 220; quoted, 207.
Maclaren, Ian, 211, 213.
Maeterlinck, 172.
Magazines, 163-166.
Malory, Thomas, "Morte d'Arthur," 196.
Marcus Aurelius, "Reflections," 7.
Marlowe, Christopher, "The Jew of Malta," 76.
Melody, 235-240.
Meredith, George, "The Ordeal of Richard Feverel," 92, 181, 208.
Metre, 227-230.
Milton, John, 108, 140, 143; "L' Allegro," 106; "Il Penseroso," 107; "Lycidas," 77; "On the Morning of Christ's Nativity," 100; quoted, 63, 113, 163.
Modernity, 169.
Molière, 140, 143.
Montaigne, 133, 140, 143.
Morbidity, 140.
Morley, John, 67.
"Mother Goose," 96, 221.
Mulock, D. M., 189.
Music, barbaric, 90; Chinese, 90.

INDEX 259

Musset, A. de, "Mlle. de Maupin," 177.

Newspapers, 162, 163.
Nordau, Max, "Degeneration," 170; quoted, 171.
Notes, use of, 84, 109.
Notoriety, 128, 172.
Novels, realistic, 209; vs. poetry, 245; with a theory, 167.
Novelty, 134.

"Old Oaken Bucket," The, 17.
Originality, 170.
Ouida, 17, 41.

Page, T. N., 211.
Pater, Walter, "Marius the Epicurean," 25.
Periodicals, 162-166.
Petrarch, 143.
Philology not the study of literature, 79.
Plato, quoted, 234.
Plutarch, letter to his wife, 50.
Poe, E. A., "Lygeia," 22; quoted, 104, 105, 237, 249; Tales, 21.
Poetry, defined, 227; form is essential, 236, 239; how different from prose, 231, 232; office in education, 223; office of, 245-252; optimism of, 248-250; origin, 5; reading of, 244; vs. novels, 245.
Pope, Alexander, 66.
Prose, how different from poetry, 231-232; language of, 231.
Public guided by the few, 10.

Quincy, Josiah, 50.

Rabelais, 133, 140.
Reade, Charles, 189.
Reading, first, 85; for amusement, 210; measure of character, 159; serious matter, 87; should be a pleasure, 71-73; test of, 86; works as units, 81.
Realism, 69, 209.
Reverence, 87.
Rhythm, 220, 221, 227-229.
Richardson, Samuel, 66.
Rossetti, D. G., 181; "Sister Helen," 119, 120.
Rousseau, "Confessions," 7.
Ruskin, John, quoted, 95.
Russell, W. Clark, 13, 211.

Sanity, 140, 174.
Schopenhauer, quoted, 63, 227.
Science vs. art, 32.
Science vs. literature, case of Darwin, 55.
Scott, Sir Walter, 189.
Sculpture, Aztec, 89; Greek, 89.
Sensationalism, 26.
Sentiment, 16, 157; defined, 15.

Sentimentality, 16, 139, 157; defined, 15.
Shakespeare, William, 3, 35, 41, 53, 58, 65, 77, 86, 92, 93, 107, 118, 124, 133, 140, 143, 145, 147, 173, 214, 216; as a classic, 152-153; condensation of, 93; "Cymbeline," 75; epithets of, 112, 231; for children, 197; "Hamlet," 81, 215; "King Lear," 81; "The Merchant of Venice," 115-118; "Othello," 81; quoted, 102, 104, 113, 114, 115, 220, 231, 239; "Sonnets," 8, 239.
Shelley, P. B., 92, 131; quoted, 254; "Stanzas Written in Dejection," etc., 17.
Shorthouse, J. H., "John Inglesant," 29.
Sienkiewicz, 182; "The Deluge," 92.
Sincerity, 12-15.
Smile, sardonic, 95.
Sophocles, 149.
Spenser, Edmund, 123, 124, 143, 197.
Standards, 141; of criticism, 161.
Steele, Sir Richard, 66.
Stephen, Leslie, 67.
Stevenson, R. L., 181; "Kidnapped," 197; quoted, 57; "Treasure Island," 27, 197.
Stockton, Frank, "The Adventures of Captain Horn," 27.
Story, happy ending of a, 215; the short, 211-214.
Stowe, Mrs. H. B., on Byron, 62.
Suckling, Sir John, quoted, 106.
Suggestion, 111-114, 118-120, 230, 235.
Suttner, Baroness von, 161.
Swift, Jonathan, 66; "Gulliver's Travels," 197.
Swinburne, A. C., 181; "Atalanta in Calydon," 228; excess of melody, 236.
Symbolism, 69.
Sympathy between reader and author, 82.

Talleyrand, quoted, 38.
Tasso, 143.
Taste a measure of character, 3.
Technical excellence, 25.
Tennyson, Alfred, 92, 155, 179, 180, 232; "Idylls of the King," 180; "In Memoriam," 7, 50; quoted, 101, 249.
Thackeray, W. M., 42, 179, 180, 189; Beatrix Esmond, 92; Colonel Newcome, 13; "Henry Esmond," 208; Major Pendennis, 201; "Pendennis," 200.
Titian, 42-43.
Tolstoi, 172, 177; "The Kreutzer Sonata," 20, 214; "War and Peace," 29.
Traill, H. D., quoted, 190.
Translations, use of, 147, 148.
Trollope, Anthony, 180, 189.

Tupper, M. F., 3.
Turgenieff, 182.

"Uncle Tom's Cabin," 160.

Vedas, The, 145.
Verlaine, 22.

"Waly, waly," 138.
Wendell, Barrett, quoted, 42.

Weyman, S. J., 211.
Whittier, J. G., 181.
Wilkins, Miss M. E., 211, 213.
Wordsworth, William, 54, 66; "The Daffodils," 17; quoted, 108, 225, 238, 239, 241, 243; "To Lucy," 13.

Zend-Avesta, The, 145.
Zola, 172, 173, 177; "L'Assommoir," 173.

The Riverside Press
CAMBRIDGE, MASSACHUSETTS, U. S. A.
ELECTROTYPED AND PRINTED BY
H. O. HOUGHTON AND CO.